Common Sense In Chess

by Emanuel Lasker

Edited by Bruce Alberston

Including Seven Additional Annotated Games
by Lasker from Hastings 1895

2007
Russell Enterprises, Inc.
Milford, CT USA

Common Sense In Chess

ISBN: 978-1-888690-40-8

Published by:
Russell Enterprises, Inc.
P.O. Box 5460
Milford, CT 06460 USA

http://www.chesscafe.com
info@chesscafe.com

Cover design by Janel Lowrance

Printed in the United States of America

Table of Contents

Acknowledgments

Thanks to Taylor Kingston for analytical endnotes and to Mark Donlan for editing at the production end. The persistence award goes to Hanon Russell and my agent Julia Lord. Without their efforts this book might never have seen the light of day. Also, thanks to Fred Wilson for analysis and general sound advice.

Standard Symbols and Abbreviations

K stands for King

Q stands for Queen

R stands for Rook

B stands for Bishop

N stands for Knight

P stands for Pawn although in practice the "P" is rarely used.

- (the dash) means "moves to"

x means "captures"

0-0 means "castles kingside"

0-0-0 means "castles queenside"

† stands for check

or mate stands for checkmate

1-0 means White wins

0-1 means Black wins

½-½ means tie game, a draw

! indicates a strong move

!! indicates an excellent, brilliant move

!? indicates an interesting but unclear move

? is a bad or questionable move

?? is a serious blunder

Editor's Introduction

by Bruce Alberston

1895 was a year of peace and prosperity. It was a time of great optimism, when advances in science and technology pointed to a future of unending progress, when all matters appeared ultimately comprehensible. The newly crowned chess champion of the world fit neatly into the period. Emanuel Lasker, then 26, had wrested the title from Steinitz the year before and was supremely self confident. For a lecture series in the spring of '95, Lasker conceived the ambitious project of reducing the game of chess to a small set of basic principles, which could then be applied to wide variety of situations. The result is *Common Sense in Chess*, long regarded as a classic both during Lasker's lifetime and for generations afterwards. It is a masterpiece of compression and exposition, and in the whole of chess literature, there is nothing that quite compares with it.

For the present reworking I have converted to algebraic notation, added diagrams, and reformatted. Editing to text is largely cosmetic and the reader can rest assured that nothing of substance has been deleted. I've fleshed out game scores, but otherwise have kept my hands off the variations. Lasker wanted his analysis short, to the point, and on the whole reliable. Readers wanting a bit more depth may avail themselves of the analytical endnotes. I have also added two chapters, on the key games of the last round of the Hastings 1895 tournament, and the other games Lasker annotated for the book of that historic event.

But the reader really wants to know not what I did, but what Lasker did. To start with, Lasker gave a series of 12 lectures in London, in the spring of 1895. These were geared to the level of the club players, or intermediate level. Later that year Lasker gathered his lecture material together and wrote it up in manuscript form to be published, retaining still, the informal, conversational tone of the lectures.

So what's in the lectures? Well, a little bit of everything. Or at least everything Lasker thought a club player should know. There's basic opening theory built around a handful of simple, easy to remember rules. There's middle game strategy and tactics, embedded in the chapters on attack and defence, and finally a long endgame section, three lectures rolled into one chapter.

The first six chapters deal with the openings. Chapter One develops fundamental principles which are then applied to the later chapters. The two sections on the Ruy Lopez, Berlin and Open Defence, as well as on the French were likely prepared beforehand. Lasker had plenty of experience with these lines, having played both sides, so he knew whereof he spoke. It's state of the art theory (for 1895), much of which had not yet percolated down to the masses.

Two other openings, the Evans Gambit and Bishop's Gambit, were at the special request of the club members. Here Lasker was on shakier ground. Gambits were disappearing from serious tournament and match play and Lasker had very little experience with either of these openings. His very first Bishop's Gambit came the following year at Nuremberg; defending as Black he lost to Charousek. The only thing to be said in mitigation is that it was the final round and Lasker had already clinched first place.

In the Evans Gambit, Lasker was somewhat more successful, having discovered (perhaps rediscovered is more accurate) a quiet little bishop move, 7...Bb6, that eliminates practically all of black's problems. This in fact was a major openings innovation, and it appears for the first time in the lecture series. When sprung on the great Evans guru, Tchigorin, later in the year, it knocked the Evans Gambit out of commission.

The chapters on attack and defence reveal Lasker's unique ability to condense matters to a single underlying principle, obstructions. It's the attacker's business to remove them, the defender's to create them. Can chess really be that simple? In Lasker's hands yes.

Finally, the three lectures on the endgame (Chapter Nine) and the three basic endgame concepts: the passed pawn, the active king, and the principle of *exhaustion*. This last has since been co-opted by the German word, *Zugzwang*. But the original notion of *corresponding squares*, here first introduced by Lasker, turns out to have a even wider application than anyone could have imagined.

Naturally, this is just the bare bones, a mere outline of Lasker's book. The impressive part is Lasker's amazing power of selection, discarding the trivial, focusing only on what is important. That and Lasker's manner of explaining things using clear, simple language. This is a rare gift. So too are Lasker's unique insights, scattered throughout the book and tossed out to his audience almost *en passant.*

Of course it's all an illusion. Lasker knew perfectly well just how difficult chess can be when played at the Master level. But then he wasn't writing for Masters. He was speaking to the average club player. And for his literary audience he adopted the same informal tone of writing, a conversational, colloquial style, a tool to put his readers at ease and to create the impression of being at the lectures.

This too is an illusion. Nobody talks as in Lasker's sentences, chock full of long subordinate clauses. There's no place to catch a breath. Missing also is the interaction with the audience, the questions and answers, and the verbal jousting. Nor would there be long blocks of moves presented without any commentary. That's dead air time and Lasker certainly knew better.

But we'll stop here. Lasker's work was not meant to be dissected. It was meant to be read, studied, and enjoyed. It's a grand *tour de force*; so enjoy and maybe learn something.

Bruce Alberston
June 2006

Author's Preface

The following is an abstract of twelve lectures given before an audience of the London chess players during the spring of 1895. It may be regarded as an attempt to deal with all parts of a game of chess by the aid of general principles. The principles laid down are deduced from considerations concerning the nature of Chess as a fight between two brains, and their conception is based on simple facts. Their practical working has been illustrated by positions adapted to the purpose, and likely to occur over the board.

It has been my aim to reduce the different rules in number as much as was compatible with clearness. They all will be found to have a remote likeness, and it would therefore not have been very difficult to reduce their number still more. Indeed, they may ultimately be united in one single leading principle, which is the germ of the theory not only of Chess, but of any kind of fight. This principle is sufficiently indicated here, but it is so general in its conception, and the difficulty of expressing the whole compass of its meaning in definite terms so enormous, that I have not ventured to formulate it. In a future work, for which the present one shall pave the way, I hope to be able to illustrate the significance of that principle, and its capacity for showing facts in their right relation to one another. For that work I have also deferred the discussion of some points which require very nice differentiation, such as all questions relating to the manoeuvering of the king and the exchange of men.

The games and positions given in this book are comparatively few, but they have been selected with care. I therefore would advise the student not to attempt to *read* the matter only, but to *study* it and sink some work into it. The rules deduced are, I believe, very plausible. This need not deceive the student who will see their significance in a clearer light if he tries to be reasonably skeptical and exacting in the matter of proofs.

As regards the analytical notes about games or openings, I have tried to be short and to the point. Analytical detail is therefore not abundant, but I think reliable. The method of enumerating *all* the variations thought possible, or probable, has been laid aside, and in its place an analysis has been given, which makes use of both the consideration of the leading variations *and* general principles. The diction and style of the work are those of a lecturer. Feeling that I have not been able to make them as perfect as I should have desired, I must ask for the lenient judgment of the reader.

I take this opportunity for expressing my hearty thanks to Professor Villin Mamery for his kind assistance in looking over the proofs.

Emanuel Lasker

Chapter One

Opening Principles

Gentlemen:

It is customary to begin with definitions, but I am sure that all of you are so well acquainted with the essential parts of the history, the rules, and the characteristics of Chess, that you will allow me to jump at once *in medias res.*

Chess has been represented, or shall I say misrepresented, as a game—that is, a thing which could not well serve a serious purpose, solely created for the enjoyment of an empty hour. If it were a game only, Chess would never have survived the serious trials to which it has, during the long time of its existence, been often subjected.

By some ardent enthusiasts Chess has been elevated into a science or an art. It is neither; but its principle characteristic seems to be—what human nature mostly delights in—a fight. Not a fight, indeed, such as would tickle the nerves of coarser natures, where blood flows and the blows delivered leave their visible traces on the bodies of the combatants, but a fight in which the scientific, the artistic, the purely intellectual element holds undivided sway.

From this standpoint, a game of Chess becomes a harmonious whole, the outlines of which I will endeavor to describe to you in this course of lectures.

The requisites in Chess are a board of sixty-four squares, and two bodies of men. We have therefore, one great advantage over the general who is to lead an army into the field—we know where to find the enemy, and the strength at his disposal. We have the gratifying knowledge that as far as material strength is concerned we shall be equal to our opponents. Nevertheless, our first step will be exactly analogous to that of a commander of an army. First of all we shall mobilize our troops, make them ready for action, try to seize the important lines and points which are yet wholly unoccupied.

This proceeding will take as rule, no more than six moves, as we shall see later on. If we should neglect to do so, our opponent would avail himself of the opportunity thus given him, would quickly assail some vital point, and ere we could rally, the battle would be finished.

Let me, in illustration of my assertions, go over some well known little games, in which mistakes and the punishment thereof are clearly traceable.

Game #1
White vs. Black
Philidor Defence

1.	e4	e5
2.	Nf3	d6
3.	Bc4	h6

Except for his last move Black has played well. He's opened lines for his two bishops and for the queen, and should now bring his knight to c6. Instead, afraid of some premature attack, he unnecessarily makes a move that does not give additional force to any of his pieces.

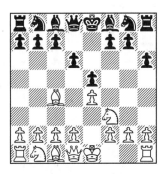

| 4. | Nc3 | Bg4 |

A mistake. The knights should be first developed, then the bishops.

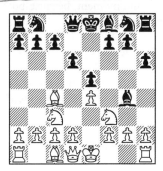

5.	Nxe5	Bxd1
6.	Bxf7†	Ke7
7.	Nd5#	

1-0

Checkmate.

Another tune to the same song:

Game #2
White vs. Black
Petroff Defence

1.	e4	e5
2.	Nf3	Nf6
3.	Nxe5	Nc6

Black evidently believes in the principle of quick development and even neglects to take White's e-pawn, in order to gain time.

4.	Nxc6	dxc6
5.	d3	Bc5
6.	Bg5	....

A mistake. He ought to guard against the threatened ...Ng4 with Be2. After the move played he is overtaken by catastrophe.

| 6. | .... | Nxe4 |

7.	Bxd8	Bxf2†
8.	Ke2	Bg4#
	0-1	

5.	Bxd5	g5
6.	Nf3	Qh5
7.	h4	....

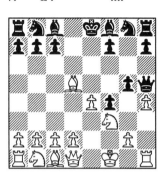

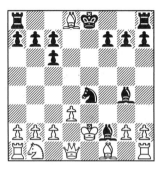

Checkmate.

Another variation:

Game #3
White vs. Black
King's Gambit

1.	e4	e5
2.	f4	exf4

White, in order to aid his development, sacrifices a pawn. Whether with good reason or not, we shall not argue for the present.

3.	Bc4	Qh4†
4.	Kf1	d5

An excellent move. Black also sacrifices a pawn, to invest it, so to say, in facilities for bringing out his pieces.

A good move which gives our rook something to do. The attack on Black's g5-pawn, however, is only an apparent one for the moment, because both the knight and the h-pawn are pinned.

7.	....	h6

He ought to develop a piece, for instance, ...Bg7. This omission will cost him the game.

8.	Bxf7†	Qxf7

Not 8...Kxf7 on account of 9. Ne5†

9.	Ne5	Qg7
10.	Qh5†	Ke7
11.	Ng6†	Kd8
12.	Nxh8	Qxh8
13.	hxg5	....

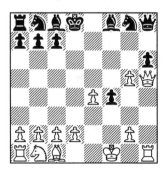

We have two pawns and an excellently placed rook for two pieces, while Black's pieces are all still at home, and his king in an unsafe position. Between fairly even players the issue of the game is therefore decided in favor of White.

Let me go over the moves which frequently occur in games of a close character.

Game #4
Fritz vs. Mason
Nuremberg, 1883
French Defence

1.	e4	e6
2.	d4	d5
3.	Nc3	Nf6
4.	Bg5	Be7

He ought to first exchange the pawns and then bring out his bishop to e7. In such manner he would obtain an almost unassailable position.

5.	Bxf6	Bxf6
6.	Nf3	0-0

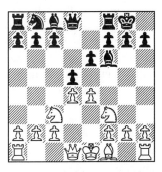

There is no necessity for him to castle so early. His first aim should be to bring his queenside into action. For instance 6...dxe4 7. Nxe4 Nd7 8. Bd3 b6 9. 0-0 Bb7, would be, although not the very best, a sufficiently safe plan for bringing his pieces out.

7.	Bd3	b6
8.	e5	Be7
9.	h4	....

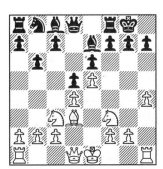

White consistently takes aim against Black's kingside. Black's queenside pieces have so little bearing upon the actual scene of battle that his game is already greatly compromised.

9.	....	Bb7

The only comparatively safe move would have been ...Ba6.

10.	Bxh7†	Kxh7
11.	Ng5†	....

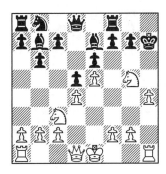

11.	....	Kg6

If instead 11...Kg8 12. Qh5 Bxg5 13. hxg5 f6 14. g6 and mate cannot be avoided.

12.	Ne2 [1]	Bxg5

11

13.	hxg5	f5

If 13...Qxg5 14. Nf4† Kf5 (15...Qxf4
16. Qh5#) 15. Qd3† Kg4 16. Qh3†
Kxf4 17. Qf3 mate.

14.	gxf6	Kf7
15.	Nf4	Rh8

To protect himself against White playing Rh7. But the defence is of no avail
as his cruel foe does not allow him a
moment's repose.

16.	Qg4!	Rxh1†

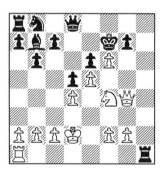

17.	Kd2	....
17.	....	gxf6

What shall he do? If 17...Rh7 18.
Qxe6† Kf8 19. Ng6 mate.

18.	Qg6†	Ke7

19.	Qg7†	Ke8
20.	Qg8†	Ke7
21.	Qxe6†	Kf8

First White drives the black king into
the most dangerous spot and then
comes the finishing stroke.

22.	Rxh1	Kg7
23.	Rh7†	Kxh7
24.	Qf7†	Kh8
25.	Ng6#	
	1-0	

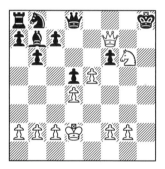

Checkmate.

If we again critically glance over the
few variations that we have gone
through, we must be struck by one fact,
namely, that the losing side had the
greater part of his army in positions
where they had no great bearing whatever upon the questions at issue. They
might have been just as well anywhere
else but on the board.

I have formulated the rules for the development of the pieces according to
my own experience over the board, and
I think, also in accordance with established facts, in the following manner:—

1. Do not move any pawns in the opening of a game but the king and queen
pawns.

2. Do not move any piece twice in the opening, but put it at once upon the right square. In my practice I have usually found it strongest to post the knights at bishop three (f3, c3 for White, c6 and f6 for Black), where they have a magnificent sway, and the king bishop somewhere on his original diagonal, if not exposed to exchange at queen bishop four (c4/c5).

3. Bring your knights out before developing the bishops, especially the queen bishop.

4. Do not pin the adverse king knight (by Bg5/Bg4) before your opponent has castled.

In regard to Rule 1 you will sometimes, especially in queenside openings, find it a better plan to advance the c-pawn two squares before obstructing it by your queen knight. This, however, is the only exception where the violation of the principles just laid down is unquestionably justified.

You will see that according to this plan the mobilization takes altogether six moves, consumed in the development of two pawns, the two knights, and the two bishops. You may be obliged to spend some of your time in the beginning of a game for the exchange of a pawn or piece, or it may be necessary to make one or two defensive moves. But the real business of development ought to be accomplished in no more than six separate moves devoted to that purpose.

Chapter Two

Ruy Lopez, Part One

Gentlemen:

We have given in our former lecture the theory of the first part of a game of Chess and have to a certain extent attempted to prove and to illustrate it. It now remains to put it to a practical test. For this purpose we shall discuss today a popular form of opening called the Ruy Lopez, from the name of the Spanish bishop who invented it. It starts out...

Game #5
White vs. Black
Ruy Lopez

1.	e4	e5
2.	Nf3	Nc6
3.	Bb5	....

Of course you will at once perceive that the threat which White's last move seems to imply, viz. Bxc6, followed by Nxe5, is only an apparent one, as Black will regain his pawn easily. We are therefore at liberty to make any developing move we please.

According to the principles of our last lecture either 3...d6, or 3...Nf6, should be done. Both of these moves very frequently *are* made, and on the whole with satisfactory results. I favor the immediate development of the knight, as 3...d6 deprives the king bishop of the possibility to occupy the line from c5.

3.	....	Nf6

White's next move may be 4. Nc3 or 4. d3 which would give him a solid and on the whole, strong game. But these variations would not present any special difficulty to Black, who would continue, for instance, with 3...d6, and afterward adopt exactly the tactics recommended in our first lecture. White has, however, other continuations at his disposal which give him a harassing attack, which Black must exercise great judgment to meet.

4.	0-0	....

What is Black to do next? According to our principles he may play either 4...Be7 or 4...Bc5, and actually either of these moves may be made without any real danger. But this is not the question at issue. The black king knight attacks the white king pawn which White has left unguarded. Is Black to accept the offer? I consider this matter at some length because it frequently presents itself in all gambits.

My answer is this: When you are conscious not to have violated the rules laid down, you should accept the sacrifice of an important pawn, as the king pawn, queen pawn, or one of the bishop pawns. If you do not, as a rule, the pawn which you have rejected will become very troublesome to you.

Do not accept the sacrifice, however, with the idea of maintaining your material advantage at the expense of development. Such a policy never pays in the end. By far the better plan is to give the pawn up after your opponent has made some exertions to gain it. By the same process, through which your opponent has achieved greater scope for his pieces, you will then always be able to recoup yourself, and as a rule, be a gainer in the bargain.

I am speaking rather authoritatively in this matter, as I cannot prove my assertions for the moment. However, I do not ask you to believe me blindly. In the course of this lecture, and in those that are to follow, enough, I trust, will be found to warrant what I said. This principle is the one amendment which I wish to add to the four rules given in the last lecture.

4.   ....   Nxe4

This move exposes Black to some danger and I do not think it would be right of me to show you only how Black gets out of it with flying colors. We shall come to a fuller understanding of the

possibilities of the position when we let Black pay the penalty for his daring.

5.   Re1   ....

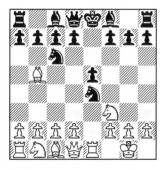

Not the best move, but one that most naturally suggests itself.

5.   ....   Nd6
To gain time by the attack on the white bishop.

6.	Nc3	Nxb5
7.	Nxe5	....

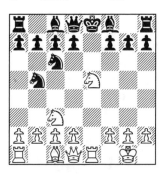

Cunning play. If Black now takes one of the knights he loses, e.g.:
(a) 7...Nxc3 8. Nxc6† Be7 9. Nxe7! Nxd1 10. Ng6† Qe7 11. Nxe7 and remains a piece ahead.
(b) 7...Nxe5 8. Rxe5† Be7 9. Nd5! 0-0 [2] 10. Nxe7† Kh8

Now see White's mode of attack which is rather instructive and of frequent occurrence. 11. Qh5 g6 — White threatened mate in two by Qxh7† etc. 12. Qh6 d6 — White mates in two. Which is the move? 13. Rh5 gxh5 14. Qf6 checkmate.

Let us now return to the original position at Black's seventh turn to move.

7.   ....   Be7

We thus intercept the dangerous file against our king and develop a piece—two great advantages.

8.	Nd5 [3]	0-0
9.	Nxc6	dxc6
10.	Nxe7†	Kh8
11.	Nxc8	Qxc8
12.	d3	Qf5
13.	Be3	h6

And Black's game is, if anything, preferable. You see how quickly White's

attack has spent itself out. But then he did not make the best of his position at move five. Let us therefore return to that point.

5.   d4   ....

We develop and attack at the same time, while our pawn cannot be taken, viz. 5...exd4 6. Re1 f5 7. Nxd4 threatening to gain a piece (among other things) by f2-f3, and should win.

5.   ....   Be7

5...Nd6 instead leads to an early exchange of queens. The resulting position is rather somewhat in favor of White, viz. 5...Nd6 6. Bxc6 dxc6 7. dxe5 Nf5 8. Qxd8† Kxd8 9. Rd1† Ke8 10. Nc3 Be7 11. h3 Be6 12. Bg5, with an occasional onslaught of the kingside pawns.

6.   Qe2   ....

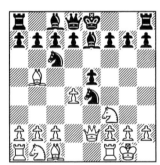

This last move is more aggressive than 6. dxe5 at once, which would allow Black time to do anything he pleases, for instance to castle at once, or to advance ...d5.

Consider the following variation as an example of what is likely to follow after 6. dxe5 d5 7. exd6 Nxd6 8. Bxc6†

16

bxc6 9. Ne5 Bb7, and in spite of his doubled pawn Black's pieces are excellently placed.

| 6. | .... | Nd6 |
| 7. | Bxc6 | bxc6 |

Not 7...dxc6 which would open the d-file to White's rook, e.g. 8. dxe5 Nf5 9. Rd1 Bd7.

Analysis: after 9...Bd7

The black d7-bishop and the queen are now so badly placed that White has an opportunity of bringing the game to a virtual finish by energetic attack: 10. e6 fxe6 11. Ne5 threatening the bishop and 12. Qh5†.

| 8. | dxe5 | Nb7 |

We have now come to a critical stage. Black's pieces have retired into safety, ready, with one single move, to occupy points of importance.

White on the contrary, has the field to himself, but he can do nothing at present, as there is no tangible object of attack. Various attempts have been made to show that White has here the superior position. I do not believe that White has any advantage, and am rather inclined to attribute the greater vitality

to the party that has kept its forces a little back.

Ere we proceed any further let us consider some sub-variations:

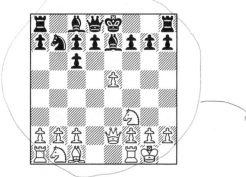

9. Nd4 0-0 10. Rd1 Qe8 11. Re1 (to prevent either ...f6 or ..d5) 11...Nc5 (not to be recommended, although in frequent use) 12. Nc3 Ba6 13. Qg4 Ne6 14. Nf5 Kh8 15. Ne4

Analysis: after 15. Ne4

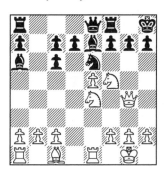

Black is quite helpless against the threat Re3 and Rh3 etc.

Or again: 9. Nd4 0-0 10. Rd1 Qe8 11. Re1 Nc5 12. Nc3 Ne6 13. Nf5 d5[4] 14. exd6 cxd6 15. Qg4 g6 16. Bh6 Ng7 17. Nxe7† Qxe7 18. Qd4 and wins at least the exchange.

These variations show that it must be Black's aim to post his king bishop on a line where he can do some effectual work, and to advance his d-pawn. From this position (after 8...Nb7), the following variations suggest themselves:

9.	Nd4	0-0
10.	Rd1	Qe8
11.	Re1	Bc5!
12.	Nb3	Bb6
13.	Nc3	d5

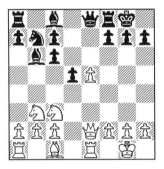

If Black has not the best of the position, at least all danger is past.

Another attempt.

9.	Nc3	0-0
10.	Nd4	Bc5
11.	Be3	Qe8
12.	f4	d6

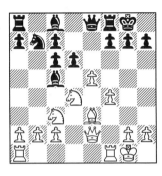

Black's pieces are again all well in play. White has, to a certain extent, compromised himself by the advance of the f-pawn.

We can now make our final judgment. The defence considered, initiated by 3...Nf6, yields, in all respects, a satisfactory game to the second player.

Chapter Three

Ruy Lopez, Part Two

Gentlemen:

Though we have established in our last lecture a line of play which will yield a good defence to the usual form of the Ruy Lopez, we may nevertheless look at others well worth noticing.

Truth derives its strength not so much from itself as from the brilliant contrast it makes with what is only apparently true. This applies especially to Chess, where it is often found that the profoundest moves do not much startle the imagination.

A defence which is frequently played is initiated in the third move by advancing the a-pawn against our bishop. I need not dwell on the point that this move is against the principles of our first lecture, just as much as 3...Nf6 is in accord with them. Neither does it, I believe, lead to an even game—an opinion which I shall attempt to substantiate in the following variations:

Game #6
White vs. Black
Ruy Lopez

1.	e4	e5
2.	Nf3	Nc6
3.	Bb5	a6

White has now the option to exchange his bishop against the adverse knight, or to retreat it. As a general rule, it is not good policy to exchange in the early stages of a game the long-reaching bishop against the knight, whose power does not extend beyond a certain circle.

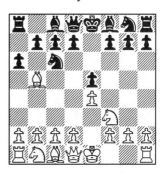

Therefore:

| 4. | Ba4 | .... |

4...d6 is not to be recommended on account of 5. d4 Bd7 6. c3 f5 7. exf5 e4 8. Ng5 with an all-round healthy position for White.

| 4. | .... | Nf6 |
| 5. | 0-0 | .... |

Both 5. Nc3 or 5. d3 would yield White a good game. However, his chances of success are greatly increased if he adopts a more dashing form of attack.

Black cannot well refuse the acceptance of the (momentary) sacrifice, as otherwise White will obtain a good position by d4 followed by e5, or else 5...d6 6. d4 b5 7. dxe5 with a good game.

5.	....	Nxe4
6.	d4	b5
7.	Bb3	....

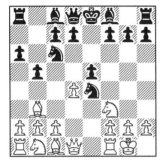

Black would be rather venturesome to take the d-pawn because White could continue with Re1 and molest the black knight, in fact finally win it.

7.	....	d5
8.	dxe5	Be6
9.	c3	....

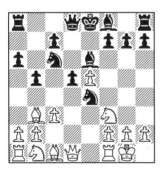

White's last is an exception to the rule to develop as quickly as possible. The game has already assumed a character of its own, which in consequence, adds to the importance of some pieces in preference to others. Our K-bishop is destined to serve as the backbone of our

attack against the black king, in the moment (which must soon arrive) that he castles on the K-side. We therefore preserve it against the possible attack of the black knights, which are driven into exposed points.

| 9. | .... | Bc5 |

e7 would also be a favorable spot for the bishop, but it seems necessary to reserve this point for the queen knight. Moreover, there is a certain want of protection on the queenside, for which you provide by putting the bishop into the rear of your pawns.

No fault is now to be found with black's *development*, all his pieces being well in play, but his pawn position on the queenside is compromised. How White will take advantage of that weakness the following will explain.

| 10. | Nbd2 | 0-0 |
| 11. | Bc2 | .... |

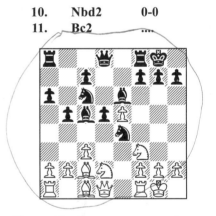

The position becomes now very instructive. Whether the twice attacked knight is removed, or exchanged, or guarded, in each case White obtains a splendid game.

Variation A

| 11. | .... | Ng5 |

12.	Nxg5	Qxg5
13.	Ne4	Qe7
14.	Nxc5	Qxc5
15.	Be3	Qe7
16.	f4	....

B1

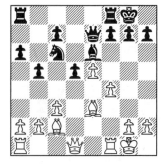

Sooner or later threatening f4-f5 with a beautiful position.

Variation B

11.	....	Nxd2
12.	Qxd2!	....

Now we threaten 13. Ng5. With 12...h6 he cannot defend as 13. Qd3 would force 12...g6 and thus the gratuitous win of the h-pawn. If 12...Be7 13. Re1 to be followed by Nd4 and then speedily f4 would give us the pull; so he plays...

12.	....	Ne7
13.	b4	Bb6
14.	Ng5	....

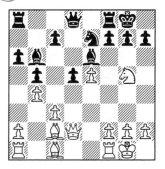

Let us consider some variations in this interesting position:

☀ Variation B1

14.	....	h6
15.	Nh7 [5]	Re8
16.	Nf6†	gxf6
17.	Qxh6	f5 [6]
18.	Bg5	....

and Black is without defence.

Variation B2

14.	....	Ng6
15.	Bxg6	hxg6
16.	Qf4	....

Threatening Qh4 etc.

16.	....	Re8
17.	Qh4	f6
18.	Qh7†	Kf8
19.	Qh8†	Bg8
20.	exf6	gxf6
21.	Nh7†	Kf7
22.	Bh6	....

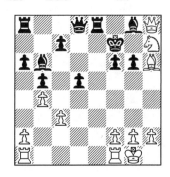

and wins.

Variation B3

14.	....	Bf5
15.	Bxf5	Nxf5

16.	Qd3	g6
17.	Qh3	h6
18.	g4	hxg5
19.	gxf5	Qe7
20.	Re1	....

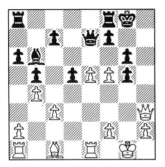

Now we threaten the advance of our f-pawn, to be followed up by Qh6. So Black can do nothing else but

20.	....	f6
21.	fxg6	fxe5
22.	Rxe5	....

regardless of expense,

22.	....	Bxf2†
23.	Kh1	Qg7 [7]
24.	Qe6†	Kh8
25.	Rxg5	....

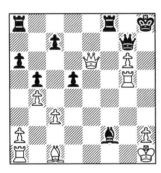

winning easily.

What must strike us most forcibly in this variation is the tremendous power

of our K-side pawns, which have swept everything before them, as a matter of fact, totally annihilated the opposing force. While at the same time Black's queenside pawns have been lazy spectators of the fight.

Let us go back again to where we left off the examination of our principal line of play.

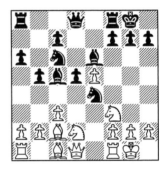

Variation C

11.	....	f5
12.	exf6	....

Also 12. Nb3 and then 13. Nbd4 would be a good continuation.

12.	....	Nxf6
13.	Ng5	Bg4
14.	Ndf3	Ne5
15.	Bf4	Nxf3†
16.	gxf3	....

| 16. | .... | Bc8 |

16...Bd7[8] would be still worse on account of the rejoinder 17. Be5.

| 17. | Qd3 | g6 |

He has no other mode of defence. If for instance 17...Ne4 18. Nxe4 dxe4 19. Qxd8 etc.

| 18. | Nxh7 | .... |

| 18. | .... | Bf5 |

Obviously, if 18...Kxh7 19. Qxg6† Kh8 20. Kh1 would speedily decide the issue.

19.	Nxf6†	Rxf6
20.	Qd2	Bxc2
21.	Bg5	....

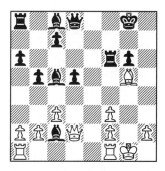

Or else 21. Qxc2 with a winning advantage.

My object in thus diving down into the depths of this position is not by any means to provide your memory with ballast. All I want to show is that the superior position will perforce become overpowering, whichever turn you may try to give to the game.

And why have we got what we termed the superior position? You see, Black's queenside pawns do not *work*, they only require protection, while White's pawns, either actively or only as potentials of future action, are contributing to White's success.

But we must not yet rest satisfied with the analysis. There may be a way of escape, at move eleven, namely:

Variation D

11.	....	Bf5
12.	Nb3	Bb6
13.	a4	....

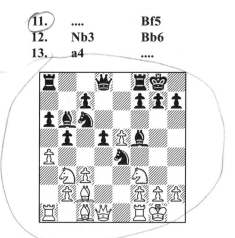

The unfortunate queenside pawns serve us again as a mark for attack. Now we threaten to exchange the pawns, then the rook, and to gain the d5-pawn.

| 13. | .... | Rb8 |

This move seems to be the only practicable reply, as otherwise, for instance, after 13...Ne7, 14. Nbd4 would become very dangerous.

14.	Nbd4	Nxd4
15.	Nxd4	Bxd4

Or if 15...Bd7 16. axb5 axb5 17. Qd3

16.	cxd4	....

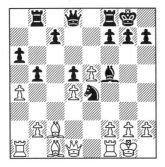

Now we have obtained our purpose. Firstly, we have the two bishops beautifully bearing down against the adverse kingside, then the black c-pawn is now kept backward by our d-pawn, and will never be able to advance.

16.	....	Bg6

Or else f3 will win a piece.

17.	axb5	axb5
18.	Ra7	c6
19.	f3	Ng5
20.	Ra6	Rc8
21.	Be3	Ne6
22.	f4	Bxc2
23.	Qxc2	Qd7

A desperate attempt to free himself by 23...c5 would fail against 24. dxc5 d4 25. Rd6 Rxc5 26. Qd3.

25.	f5	Nd8
26.	Qf2	....

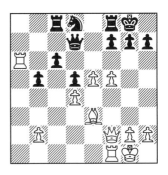

We now want our most powerful piece on the K-side.

25.	....	Kh8
26.	Qh4	Qb7

He must, after all, try to get something out of his Q-side.

27.	f6 [9]	g6
28.	Qh6	Ne6
29.	Ra3 [10]	Rg8
30.	Bd2	Nf8
31.	Bb4	....

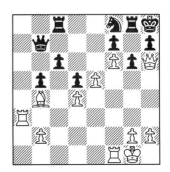

and Black is quite helpless.

Again I beg to draw your attention to the difference in power exerted by the white and the black pawns. Taken all round you will perhaps agree with me when I declare that Black, by choosing the defence 3...a6 to the Ruy Lopez, unnecessarily damages his queenside pawns, while the development of his pieces gives him no compensation for that disadvantage.

To relieve your chess nerves from the tension which they must have undergone today, allow me to introduce as a finale, a more pleasing matter. In my match with Mr. Steinitz, that master chose, for a long while, a somewhat close defence to the Ruy Lopez, beginning with 3...d6. The game usually ran as follows:

Game #7
White vs. Black
Ruy Lopez

1.	e4	e5
2.	Nf3	Nc6
3.	Bb5	d6
4.	d4	Bd7
5.	Nc3	Nge7
6.	Bc4	....

Threatening of course Ng5.

6.	....	exd4
7.	Nxd4	....

Now it seems that Black, in order to keep White's queen at bay, has a good way of developing his KB by means of ...g6 followed by ...Bg7, where the bishop would certainly have an excellent diagonal. This little plan, however, was never executed by Mr. Steinitz, for the reason appearing in what follows. If

7.	....	g6
8.	Bg5	....

In order to take possession of the diagonal which Black attempts to occupy.

8.	....	Bg7
9.	Nd5	....

Attack and counter attack.

9.	....	Bxd4

Anything else would be clearly disadvantageous. Black, of course, is now under the expectation that White will continue with 10. Nxe7 when 10...Bxb2 would allow Black to get out of danger. But White has a more efficient move at his disposal.

10.	Qxd4!	....

This is very awkward for Black. If now 10...Nxd4 11.Nf6† Kf8 12. Bh6 checkmate. So nothing remains but to castle.

10.	....	0-0
11.	Nf6†	Kh8
12.	Ng4†	Nxd4
13.	Bf6†	Kg8
14.	Nh6#	

1-0

Chapter Four

Evans Gambit

Gentlemen:

The Evans Gambit, which in accordance with your desire I have chosen tonight as subject of discussion, is constituted by these four moves:

Game #8
White vs. Black
Evans Gambit

1.	e4	e5
2.	Nf3	Nc6
3.	Bc4	Bc5
4.	b4	.. ..

There is no necessity for Black to accept the offer of the pawn. On the contrary, if he retires his bishop to b6 in reply, he will, as White's last move has in no way furthered his development, gain a small but distinct advantage in position. The play which would then ensue will be of the following character:

4.	....	Bb6
5.	a4	a6
6.	c3	Nf6
7.	d3	d6
8.	0-0	Ne7

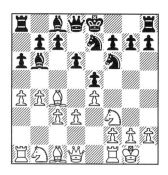

soon to be followed by ...c6 and ...d5.

Black's pieces are all well placed, no matter whether White castles at his eighth turn to move, or defers that yet for some time. If White therefore sacrifices a pawn by giving the gambit, Black sacrifices the sure prospect of positional advantage by taking it.

The idea of the gambit is very obvious. We want to continue, if **4...Bxb4** (or ...Nxb4), with

5.	c3	....

and later on proceed with the advance of the d-pawn, so as to obtain a very strong centre and to open several lines for the attack of the pieces.

The bishop can retire to either c5, a5, e7, to his own square f8, or to d6, where he is not as badly placed as at first sight appears. The best players favor ...Ba5 or ...Bc5, with a preference for the former. If we retire to c5 the bishop may be attacked again by 6. d4, while, on the contrary, ...Ba5 counteracts that advance. On the other hand, the bishop at a5 will take away from the queen knight an important point, from where he might attack the white king bishop. But taken all around,

| 5. | .... | Ba5 |

seems to be the preferable move.

White now has two formidable continuations.

| 6. | d4 | .... |

naturally suggests itself first, although it is not of such lasting effect as another move which we shall consider later on. Black will answer

| 6. | .... | exd4 |
| 7. | 0-0 | dxc3 |

The weakest point in Black's camp is the f7-pawn, so we follow up our attack by

| 8. | Qb3 | .... |

Black can reply with either ...Qe7 or ...Qf6. From e7 the queen has hardly any move that is not commanded by White's pieces, therefore

| 8. | .... | Qf6 |
| 9. | e5 | .... |

in the expectation of embarrassing Black's development, as neither the d-pawn nor the f-pawn can advance for the present without being taken, with the effect that all lines are opened up to our pieces.

| 9. | .... | Qg6 |
| 10. | Nxc3 | Nge7 |

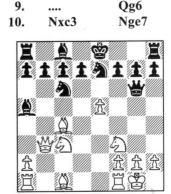

In this position we already see that White's attacking moves are pretty well exhausted. He has only a very unsatisfactory continuation.

| 11. | Ba3 | .... |

Which gives to the bishop a long diagonal merely in exchange for another one.

This position has been the subject of analysis for many decades and several variations have been found which seem to leave Black with a comparatively safe king position and a pawn ahead. None of the continuations given seem to be superior to the one that follows.

11.	....	Bxc3

(This move was suggested by Mr. Lord during the lecture.)

12.	Qxc3	b6
13.	Bd3	Qh6

Not 13...Qh5 as 14. Bxe7 Kxe7 15. e6 might follow.

14.	Rfd1	Bb7

and it is difficult to see in which way White will make good his minus of two pawns.

This line of play, the so called compromised defence of the Evans Gambit, leads sometimes to very brilliant combinations. Let me give you an instance of this at move 11 of our principal variation.

11.	....	0-0

12.	Rad1	Re8
13.	Ne4	Qxe4
14.	Bxf7†	Kf8
15.	Bg8	d5 [11]
16.	exd6	Nxg8

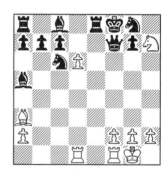

17.	Ng5	Qf5
18.	Qf7†	Qxf7
19.	Nxh7#	
		1-0

Instead of 6. d4, the greatest connoisseur of the Evans, Mr. Tchigorin, favors 6. 0-0, with the object of maintaining his centre. It cannot be doubted that this line of play is more in keeping with the original idea of the gambit.

Black, in accordance with the principles laid down in lecture 1, must either play his d-pawn or his king knight. It is usually the best policy when you are subject to a violent attack to move the d-pawn, and when you are the aggressive party to develop your pieces first.

In the position before us

6.	0-0	d6

appears therefore to be the allowed sounder play.

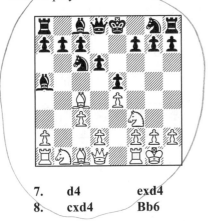

7.	d4	exd4
8.	cxd4	Bb6

leads to the "normal position" of the Evans.

The five pawns that White has gathered on his king's wing against Black's four, exert a considerable amount of pressure on the black pieces, the more so as Black will be obliged to leave his king on the dangerous side. It is true that Black may establish three pawns to one on the other wing, but then it will take him a great deal of time to force the fighting on that side, while White's pieces will soon be in direction and ready for assault.

Various continuations have recently been recommended as best for White, but it seems to me that the old way of playing is as good as any. The line of play usually followed by the old masters is

9.	d5	Na5
10.	Bb2	Ne7

11.	Bd3	f6
12.	Nc3	0-0

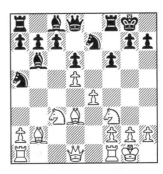

It is not my intention to analyze the position by the method usually followed, of simply enumerating all possible variations. Such analysis, unless it is very thorough, I contend, is quite useless. It certainly, as the experience of many centuries indisputably shows, would by no means exclude the possibility of committing grave errors, and it usually puts into obscurity the points of view from which the essential characteristics of the position may be deduced.

Without going into details, this much is certain, either:

(a) Black will advance his f-pawn to f5, or
(b) He will initiate an attack on the queenside with ...c5, ...a6, ...Bc7, ...b5 etc., or
(c) He will be content to break up White's strong centre by ...c6.

There is indeed no other *plan de campagne* to follow.

As regards the first point, it is easily seen that such an advance would not increase the defensive strength of Black's position. It would open the diagonal of the white QB, the point e4 to the white knights (after the exchange of pawns), and probably facilitate the joint attack of the white f-pawn and g-pawn.

(b) This was the plan of defence, or rather counter attack, in Anderssen's tierce. White will obtain the advantage in the following manner:

13.	Kh1	Ng6
14.	Nd2	c5
15.	f4	a6
16.	Ne2	Bc7
17.	Nf3	b5
18.	f5	Ne5
19.	Nf4	....

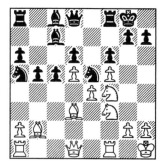

This will represent pretty accurately the state of affairs ten or twelve moves after the normal position has been arrived at. It takes at least seven moves to bring the black pawns to their destination. In the meantime White is free to advance his g-pawn in two steps to g5, and to open up a pernicious attack against Black's kingside.

(c) White's policy will be exactly as in (b), to advance his f-pawn. If Black exchanges the c-pawn against the d5-pawn, the e4-pawn will retake, and the black queen knight will be unfavorably situated. Black has in this variation practically no chance of winning, in spite of his extra pawn, while the attack of White is very lasting and dangerous.

It seems that the normal position will yield to White much better chances of winning than it will to Black.

If you want to simplify matters, I advise you to play

7.   ....   Bb6

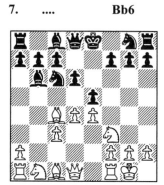

at once, with the object of converting your extra material into positional advantage. If then 8. dxe5 dxe5 9. Qxd8†
Nxd8 10. Nxe5 Nf6.

Analysis: after 10...Nf6

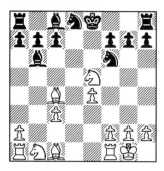

Black's solid pawns and good, sound development will make it hard for White to keep up the equilibrium as his a-pawn, and more so the c-pawn, require constant care.

If, on the other hand, 8. dxe5 dxe5 9. Qb3 Qf6 10. Bd5 Nge7 11. Bg5 Qg6 12. Bxe7 Kxe7 13. Bxc6 Qxc6 14. Nxe5 Qe6 15. Qa3† c5 (or 15...Kf6)

Analysis: after 15...c5

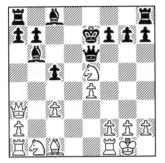

with two bishops, a healthy development of forces, and a solid position.

One of the finest games on record was played at a time when the analysis of the Evans Gambit was not yet far advanced. It has been named "The Evergreen Partie." The leader of the white forces was Professor Anderssen.

Game #9
Anderssen vs. Dufresne
Offhand, Berlin, 1852
Evans Gambit

1.	e4	e5
2.	Nf3	Nc6
3.	Bc4	Bc5
4.	b4	Bxb4
5.	c3	Ba5
6.	d4	exd4
7.	0-0	d3

A now obsolete defence.

8.	Qb3	Qf6
9.	e5	Qg6
10.	Ba3	Nge7
11.	Re1	b5

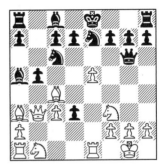

12.	Bxb5	Rb8
13.	Qa4	Bb6
14.	Nbd2	Bb7
15.	Ne4	Qf5
16.	Bxd3	Qh5
17.	Nf6†	gxf6
18.	exf6	Rg8
19.	Rad1	....

One of the most subtle and profound moves on record.

19.	....	Qxf3
20.	Rxe7†	Nxe7
21.	Qxd7†	....

Grand!

21.	....	Kxd7
22.	Bf5†	Kc6
23.	Bd7#	

1-0

If at move 20 Black continues 20...Kd8, then 21. Rxd7† Kc8 22. Rd8† Nxd8 23. Qd7† and mates in two more moves.

Chapter Five

King's Bishop's Gambit

Gentlemen:

According to the request you made to me last Monday, we shall consider to-day the King's Bishop's Gambit, which as you do know, is constituted by these moves:

1.	e4	e5
2.	f4	exf4
3.	Bc4	....

If I remind you of Rule 3 you will admit that the development of the bishop is not in accordance with our fundamental principles. Actually the move of the king knight to f3 would be far stronger, as it leads to a fairly even game, while the King Bishop Gambit should be lost to the first player.

The defence will, before all, disturb the quiet course of White's development, by

3.	....	Qh4†

to which White is bound to answer with...

4.	Kf1	....

According to the principles of development, either the d-pawn or one of the knights should now move. White is threatening to bring forth an enormous force in no more than three moves, to bear on the centre of the board, namely, Nf3, Nc3, d4. Black dare not quietly submit to that, as for the moment his queen is exposed to danger. To keep the white king in his unsound position, to spoil the plan of White, and to aid the quick development of Black's forces, the best policy is the most aggressive one, that is, the one initiated by the sacrifice of the d-pawn.

4.	....	d5
5.	Bxd5	....

Now, before anything else is undertaken...

5.	....	g5!

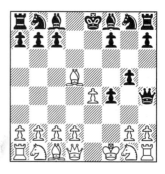

Our bishops have two long lines; our knights have only one move to make to occupy points of importance, and to add to the firmness of our position. We can, therefore, spare the time for this advance of g-pawn, destined to protect our f4-pawn against all possible attack,

32

and to render the kingside unsafe for White's pieces.

6.	**Nf3**	**Qh5**
7.	**h4**	**Bg7**

An excellent reply. The bishop not only protects the rook, but guards the two centre points, d4 and e5.

8.	**d4**	**h6**
9.	**Kg1**	**Qg6**
10.	**Nc3**	**Ne7**

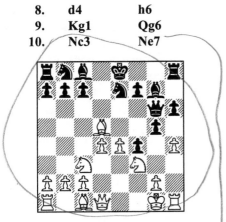

So far, everything went all right, because White consistently played for the development of his minor pieces. Now it becomes apparent that the white queen rook is awkwardly placed, and the queen bishop no less. The king position need not give any anxiety, but the queen has somehow no good prospects of serving her cause. At the same time, Black is quite safe—there is only one weak point in his camp, the f-pawn—and any possible attacks of the white minor pieces in the centre are obviated by the clever sacrifice of the 4th move.

11.	**Qd3**	**....**

Preparatory to Bd2.

11.	**....**	**c6**

12.	**Bb3**	**Bg4!**

Here the queen bishop has a splendid position safe from all possible attack by inferior pieces and with h5 as a safe retreat.

13.	**Bd2**	**Nd7**
14.	**Kf2**	**0-0-0**

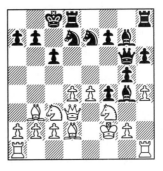

All the weakness of the white game becomes now at once apparent. His e- and d-pawns are exposed to the most direct attack of the hostile rook and knights, and king bishop. Try what he may the day is gone. Black threatens 15...Bxf3 and 16...Ne5.

If 15. Ne2 Nc5 wins easily. If 15. hxg5 hxg5 16. Rxh8 Bxh8 the danger is not obviated.

If finally 15. Qc4 Bxf3! 16. gxf3 Ne5 17. dxe5 Rxd2† 18. Ke1 Rhd8 19. Qxf7 Qxf7 20. Bxf7 Bxe5 21. Bb3 Bxc3 22. bxc3 Ng6, followed by ...Ne5, is at least *one* way of obtaining a great advantage.

Let us return to move 11 and vary White's play.

11.	**e5**	**c6**
12.	**Be4**	**Bf5**
13.	**Qe2**	**Nd7**
14.	**Bxf5**	**Nxf5**

White is obliged to undertake some kind of attack, or Black will castle queenside, and the breakdown of White's centre will be practically certain.

| 15. | Ne4 | g4 |

Now at last this advance is justified, because the d-pawn has lost its protection by the queen.

| 16. | Nd6† | Kf8 [12] |
| 17. | Nxf5 | gxf3 |

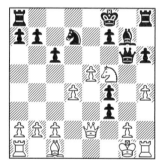

And wins a piece. If instead 17. h5 gxf3 or 17. Ne1 Nxd6 18. exd6 Bxd4† and should win.

We must therefore come to the conclusion that the King Bishop Gambit is unsound. I will not pretend that there is any right or wrong in Chess from an ethical standpoint, but by what right should White, in an absolutely even position, such as after move one, when both sides have advanced their e-pawns, sacrifice a pawn, whose recapture is quite uncertain, and open up his kingside to attack? And then follow up this policy by leaving the check of the black queen open? None whatever!

The idea of the gambit, if it has any justification, can be only to lure Black into the too violent and hasty pursuit of his attack. If, therefore, we can obtain by sound and consistent play the superiority of position, common sense triumphs over trickery, and rightly so.

When the analytical and theoretical knowledge of Chess was not so far advanced as at the present time, famous players frequently chose the lively forms of development which are the outcome of gambits. One of these games, though unsound in the highest degree, has been of such exceptionally brilliant character that it was honored by the players of the time with a special name. We know it as "The Immortal Partie."

Game #10
Anderssen vs. Kieseritzky
Offhand, London, 1851
King's Gambit

1.	e4	e5
2.	f4	exf4
3.	Bc4	Qh4†
4.	Kf1	b5
5.	Bxb5	Nf6
6.	Nf3	Qh6
7.	d3	Nh5
8.	Nh4	c6
9.	Nf5	Qg5

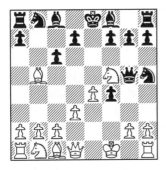

10.	g4	Nf6
11.	Rg1	cxb5
12.	h4	Qg6
13.	h5	Qg5
14.	Qf3	Ng8
15.	Bxf4	Qf6
16.	Nc3	Bc5
17.	Nd5	....

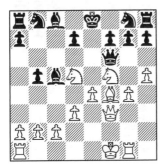

I have not dwelt on the constant violation of principle by Black. The consequence of his imaginative schemes is that none of his pieces are developed, and here White could have smashed Black up by advancing first 17. d4.

17.	....	Qxb2
18.	Bd6[13]	....

A fine coup.

18.	....	Bxg1
19.	e5	...

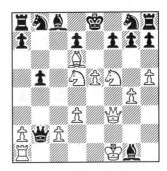

Obstructing the line from a1 to g7. A glorious finish.

19.	...	Qxa1†
20.	Ke2	Na6
21.	Nxg7†	Kd8
22.	Qf6†	Nxf6
23.	Be7#	
		1-0

Checkmate.

Chapter Six

French Defence

Gentlemen:

As you have expressed the desire to have one of the close openings discussed, I have chosen tonight the popular and important French Defence, which arises when Black replies to White's 1.e4 with 1...e6.

1.   e4   e6

This defence had for a long time the reputation of leading to a dull kind of game. In later years it has been found that it gives opportunities for a great many violent attacks of a character which it is difficult to obtain in any other opening.

The difference between black's first move ...e6 and the other ...e5, commonly chosen, is twofold. The pawn at e6 blocks the long diagonal of the black queen bishop reaching up to h3, which is, I might say, almost naturally open to him. On the other hand, in the ordinary games which open with 1. e4 e5, the white king bishop can take up a very strong diagonal from c4, pointing toward the initially weakest point in black's camp, the square f7. This line also is obstructed.

These two peculiarities give to the French Defence a character of its own, which, with good play on the part of White, it should never lose.

The move which gives the white pieces as much freedom as can be obtained in one single move, is...

2.   d4   ....

And just so on the part of Black.

2.   ....   d5

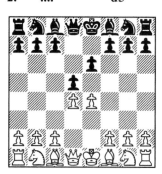

As early as this opinions greatly differ as to the best continuation to be chosen by White. The attack has namely the choice—

(a) To sacrifice the e-pawn.
(b) To exchange it.
(c) To advance it.
(d) To guard it.

(a) May be at once dismissed. If we play 3. Nf3 dxe4 4. Ng5, this may lead to a tricky game, but with sound and energetic play on the part of Black, a great advantage ought to accrue to the second player.

(c) is equally inadvisable, as the early advance of the pawns unbacked by pieces always is. This may be the line of play to follow—

3.	e5	c5
4.	c3	Nc6
5.	Nf3	Qb6
6.	Be2	Nge7
7.	0-0	Nf5

or

5.	f4	Qb6
6.	Nf3	Bd7
7.	b3	Nh6
8.	Be3	Nf5
9.	Bf2	cxd4

And if

10.	cxd4	Bb4†

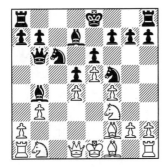

You see White comes, without compensation, into great difficulties.

(b) The exchange of pawns in the third move

3.	exd5	exd5

leads to a very even game, in which the advantage of the first move counts for very little. The game might go on...

4.	Nf3	Nf6
5.	Bd3	Bd6
6.	0-0	0-0
7.	Bg5	Be6
8.	Nbd2	Nbd7
9.	Re1	Re8
10.	Ne5	Nf8

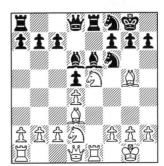

or

10.	c3	Nf8
11.	Qc2	c6
12.	Re2	Qc7
13.	Bxf6	gxf6
14.	Rae1	Ng6
15.	g3	....

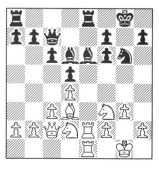

When the advantage of the doubled rooks on the open file is counterbalanced by the strong position of the two black bishops. And Black may even have, on account of the somewhat questionable exchange at move thirteen, the superior game.

A game well worth knowing in the exchange variation of the French is the one played by Blackburne vs. Englisch.

Game #11
Englisch vs. Blackburne
London, 1883
French Defence

1.	e4	e6
2.	d4	d5
3.	exd5	exd5
4.	Nf3	Nf6
5.	Bd3	Bd6
6.	0-0	0-0
7.	Nc3	Nc6

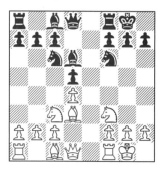

8.	Bg5	Bg4
9.	Bxf6	Qxf6

White is greedy to win a pawn and voluntarily exchanges bishop vs. pinned knight—always a great mistake.

10.	Nxd5	Qh6
11.	h3	Nxd4

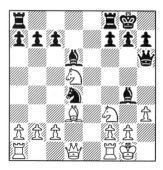

and Black (Blackburne) won easily, as White's king position is exposed.

12.	Be2	Nxf3†
13.	Bxf3	Bxh3
14.	Re1	Be6
15.	g3	Rad8
16.	Qe2	Bxd5
17.	Bxd5	Bxg3
18.	Be4	Rd2
19.	Qxd2	Bh2†

0-1

The want of *finesse* in variation (b) is accounted for by the pawn position. The pawn at d4 takes away a good square from the king knight; it blocks the line of the bishop from e3 to a7, or from c3 to g7; it further obstructs the d-file. If the two pawns on the d-file could by some means be exchanged, the position would assume a very different character. As it is, they are never to be got rid of, unless with the friendly assistance of your opponent.

(d) The strongest move that comes under this heading is 3. Nc3. A custom has lately sprung up of posting this knight at d2, where it obstructs the queen bishop and the queen. A good reply against such sickly policy is always to open up all lines quickly; for instance, in the given case to advance 3...c5.

To the move actually chosen

3.	Nc3	....

Black's answer is as a rule

3.	....	Nf6

Now most players choose as continuation

4.	Bg5	....

A move unquestionably against the rules of development, to which Black ought to reply by

4.	....	dxe4
5.	Nxe4	Be7
6.	Bxf6	gxf6
7.	Nf3	f5
8.	Ng3	c5

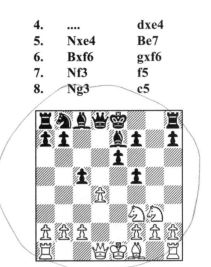

And Black will have a very good game.

The better play is the more audacious one,

4.	e5	Nfd7
5.	f4	....

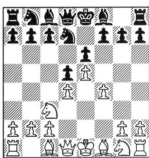

According to one of Steinitz's principles, which is, whenever you advance your pawn to e5, back it up by f4 as soon as possible.

5.	....	c5
6.	dxc5	....

This exchange of pawns is imperative. In former years White invariably tried, in close games, to keep his pawn at d4, backing it up by c3. This policy has the two great disadvantages that it leaves a weak pawn at d4 open to attack, and that it opens a file (the c-file) for the intervention of the black rooks.

6.	....	Bxc5
7.	Qg4	0-0
8.	Bd3	Nc6
9.	Nf3	....

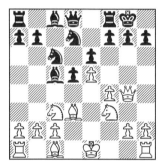

White threatens the sacrifice so common in close games, that of the bishop against the h7-pawn.

9.	....	f5
10.	Qh3	Nb4
11.	g4 [14]	....

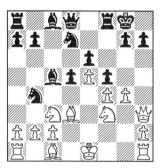

White has only *one* aim—to make play on the kingside, while the development of the black queen bishop is yet unaccomplished. He therefore does not lose any time by advancing the a-pawn,

and has now a fine attacking game. Assume for instance

11.	....	Nxd3†
12.	cxd3	Nb6
13.	d4	Bb4
14.	Bd2	Nc4
15.	a3	Nxd2
16.	Kxd2	....

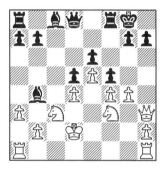

And the white game is altogether preferable. Or

11.	.. ..	Nb6
12.	a3	Nxd3†
13.	cxd3	Bd7
14.	b4	Be7
15.	Nd4	

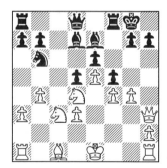

To make another attempt

11.	.. ..	Qb6
12.	gxf5	Nxd3†
13.	cxd3	Rxf5

14.   Nxd5

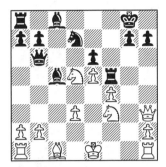

and should win.[15]

If then Black is reduced at move ten to the necessity

10.   ....   h6

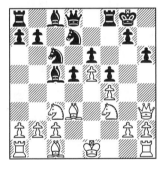

White can, nevertheless, pursue the policy of aggression by immediately advancing the g-pawn.

10.   g4   ....

To take advantage of the opportunity thus offered of opening up the adverse kingside.

Black may strengthen his defence at move six...

6.   ....   Nc6
7.   a3   Bxc5

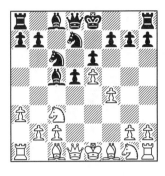

The pawn must be taken now as otherwise b4 will save it. To capture with the knight (...Nxc5) does not appear to be superior, as the knight is not very happily placed at c5, and obstructs the king bishop somewhat.

8.   Qg4   0-0

Here Black may defend himself by 8...g6, when a very difficult game will ensue, in which, however, the black kingside pawns will furnish White with good objects of attack.

9.   Bd3   a6

It is difficult to suggest a different line of play. Black must do something to bring White's queenside under pressure, as otherwise White gratuitously obtains a good kingside attack. The advance of the a-pawn and the b-pawn seem to be the only means of accomplishing that purpose.

10.   Nf3   ....

threatening Bxh7†.

10.   ....   f5
11.   Qh3   b5 [16]
12.   g4   g6
13.   Qg3   ....

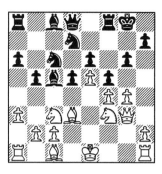

A very important manoeuvre, but it is difficult to say if this move, or Qg2, will, in the end, prove superior.

| 13. | .. .. | Kh8 |

Again, it is hard to find out better play. The threat is to obtain a passed e-pawn by gxf5.

| 14. | h4 |

with a first rate attack.

I think you will agree with the proposition that I have to lay down, viz., that 3. Nc3 subjects the defence to a difficult game. As a good reply to 3. Nc3 I advise you to choose the following continuation

| 3. | ... | dxe4 |

| 4. | Nxe4 | Nf6 |

5.	Ng3	c5
6.	Nf3	Nc6
7.	Be3	Qb6

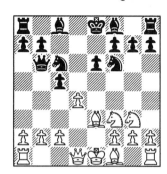

or

5.	Bd3	c5
6.	dxc5	Bxc5
7.	Nxc5	Qa5†
8.	c3	Qxc5
9.	Be3	Qc7
10.	Nf3	Nc6
11.	0-0	b6

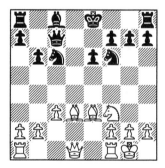

It is dangerous to castle into the two bishops' diagonals, so Black first brings out ...Bb7, then ...Rd8, and waits with moving his king until White has spent some of his accumulated "potential force" (gathered in the centre).

You may vary your tactics at move five, by playing **5....Nc6 6. c3 e5** with a good game for Black.

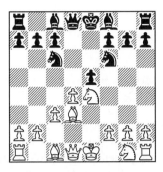

One word about close games in general. The rules of quick development as laid down in lecture one require *one* amendment, viz., do not obstruct your queen bishop pawn by your queen knight (unless you wish to open the game at once by e4/e5), and advance that pawn as early as you can to c4/c5.

After the Easter holidays we shall discuss the general principles of the remaining parts of the game, when much that has been said hitherto will obtain a different and a deeper meaning.

Chapter Seven

The Attack

Gentlemen:

So far we have considered the first part of a game of chess, called the opening, usually embracing about a dozen moves. The object of development is, as we have seen, to get the pieces into action, and to place them on favorable lines, in order to have them at hand when you intend to make them "work." The process of making pieces in Chess do something useful (what ever it may be) has received a special name: it is called the attack.

The attack is that process by means of which you remove obstructions. That is so in every fight, whether it be a battle, or a fight with swords, or a boxing encounter, this definition will always apply.

Let us compare the game of Chess to some other fight—for instance a battle. Two armies opposite each other are attempting to destroy, or at least to frighten each other. The armies, if about even in numbers, and also as far as favorable position is concerned, will each have a superiority in some quarter which will enable them not only to hold their opponents there in check, but also to drive them out of their position.

Three things determine whether an attack should be made, and if so, in which manner. First of all the proportion of the attacking force to that directly opposing it in numbers; secondly, the nature of the surroundings; thirdly, the

relation of the forces engaged to the rest of the army.

The third consideration will influence the *time* in which the attack must be executed, whether rapidly (if the advent of reserve force must under all circumstances be avoided) or step by step. In other words, it determines whether we should make it our object to economize in time, or in material force at our disposal.

The surroundings will in part add to the defensive strength of our opponents, and in part take away from it. Their character will determine which part of the hostile force is exposed to the effect of our weapons, and which is shielded; where we can advance with comparative safety, and which part of the ground we have to traverse rapidly. In other terms, which are weaknesses to be assailed, and which are strong points toward which to advance.

The first consideration will tell us whether, after we have gained, by the methodical destruction of the obstacles in our way, a position of advantage, we are able to destroy or drive away the opposing force; or whether the object of our attack, if obtained, is a sufficient compensation for the lives sacrificed. If in any kind of fight, the rules for attack are laid down, the three things mentioned must be studied.

In Chess the soldiers are the men and the general is the mind of the player. If anything that is subject to the possibility of an attack be a weak point, all men, and especially the king and the heavy pieces (queen and rooks) would be such; we shall, however, call a weakness only such pieces, or group of pieces, as in proportion to their importance have a defect in defensive strength, for instance: a queen that has only a very limited range of action, or a pawn that cannot advance nor yet be protected by other pawns.

A weak point is a *square*—not necessarily occupied—which can only be attacked by heavy pieces like the queen or the rooks. So that pawns, knights, and bishops, or eventually also rooks protected by other men, are there quite safe. Our opponent's weak points we shall name strong points, speaking from our point of view. If we can occupy a strong point by one of our pieces, which has from there a large sphere of action, the battle is often half decided in our favor.

Obstructions in Chess are pieces of minor importance which intercept the lines of action of our men. It is, as a rule, easier to remove them when they are hostile men, because we may threaten them by so many of our own pieces that we can finally safely capture them; it is different when for instance, one of our own pawns, blocked by one of the pawns or pieces of the enemy, stands in our way. And worse still when this pawn is isolated. The only way of removing it by force consists then usually in placing a piece under the protection of this pawn and forcing the exchange of that piece.

Let us now consider the initial position. The ultimate object of every attack in Chess is given beforehand—it is the capture by force of the hostile king. For that purpose we must command nine squares, the eight around the king and the one he occupies. We can reduce that number only by driving the king to the edge of the board, or by forcing his own pieces to obstruct his escape.

Finally, the check-giving piece must not be liable to capture, nor must any of the hostile pieces be able to intercept its line of attack. This is the "work to be done," and it is enormous considering the large amount of force gifted with capacity to capture and obstruct at the enemy's disposal. This task is still made more difficult by the other one which you have to perform—to protect your own king against your opponent's assaults.

The Chess world went about the task thus voluntarily undertaken and attempted to solve the problem involved by the humanly most direct method; it simply tried it, piling variation on variation, correcting and re-correcting them, for say two thousand years. Many beautiful games were played and startling discoveries made, but the real problem was never solved.

And why, may we ask, have for so long a time the exertions of the best brains of the human race continually failed? There is one answer whose cogency is irresistible, an answer whose truth seems to be proved by experience beyond doubt, viz., there *is* no solution. And for this reason. The resources on each side are so evenly balanced that the trifling advantage of the first move is not sufficient to force the defence to resignation.

This admitted, we must begin, before entering upon our task, with the supposition that the initial position has been differentiated to such an extent that the win of the game becomes possible to the one or the other party. After having granted this much the problem is transformed and it assumes the following shape: the balance of position and forces has at least been partly disturbed and to checkmate the king of the inferior force becomes a feasible achievement.

Whether a nearly balanced position allows a forced win to one or the other party depends usually on the slightest differences, so much so indeed, that it would be a hopeless undertaking to search for certain rules, or a mathematical formula that would give you its solution without the application of intellectual power in each special case. The question involved is of such a complicated nature that the only way to obtain an answer is to divide the board into parts, to analyze the partial questions by the experimental method, and to finally draw the sum total of all the answers.

Now, given a position in Chess where, on the one wing (for instance, the kingside), we have the superiority, on another (the queenside or the centre) we may be at a disadvantage, but where on the whole, our advantage is prevailing, in what manner are we to make capital out of that superiority?

The answer depends of course on the analysis of the position. But if this analysis is methodical it will greatly acquire clearness and sharpness, and the mental labor required will be reduced to a minimum.

The moves in Chess are of three kinds, they are either

(a) Developing, i.e. bringing new force into play.

(b) Attacking, i.e. making pieces threaten the hostile men, give a check, threaten a checkmate, etc. In other words, making pieces *do* something, or *work*.

(c) Serving defensive purposes, i.e. giving protection to a weak point, obstructing an important line, etc. In other words, *undoing* the work of the hostile men.

What kind of move is required is determined by the exigencies of the position. If you have a large superiority of force in a quarter where the enemy has important weaknesses, like the king or the queen in a bad position, etc., you must assail quickly. Every one of your moves must be intended to do much. Your reserve force must be made useful for the attack with as much gain of time as possible—by attacking, for instance, some weaknesses while on the way—and the reserve force of the opponent must be kept back, if possible, by obstructions that you can place in their way (think of Morphy's pawn sacrifices for that purpose). The devices are manifold, but the variations, on account of the many forced moves on the part of the defence, are usually few, and therefore subject to direct analysis. Of such attacks we say that their "pace" is quick.

All the games given, especially the French Defence of the previous lecture, have contained attacks of quick pace.

Here follows another.

Game #12
Lasker vs. Bauer
Amsterdam, 1889
Bird's Opening

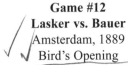

1.	f4	d5
2.	e3	Nf6
3.	b3	e6
4.	Bb2	Be7
5.	Bd3	b6
6.	Nc3	Bb7
7.	Nf3	Nbd7
8.	0-0	0-0
9.	Ne2	c5
10.	Ng3	Qc7
11.	Ne5	Nxe5
12.	Bxe5	Qc6
13.	Qe2	a6

14.	Nh5	Nxh5
15.	Bxh7†	Kxh7
16.	Qxh5†	Kg8
17.	Bxg7	Kxg7
18.	Qg4†	Kh7
19.	Rf3	e5
20.	Rh3†	Qh6
21.	Rxh6†	Kxh6
22.	Qd7	Bf6
23.	Qxb7	Kg7
24.	Rf1	Rab8
25.	Qd7	Rfd8
26.	Qg4†	Kf8
27.	fxe5	Bg7

28.	e6	Rb7
29.	Qg6	f6
30.	Rxf6†	Bxf6
31.	Qxf6†	Ke8
32.	Qh8†	Ke7
33.	Qg7†	

1-0

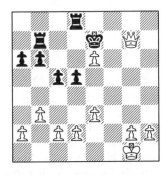

When your superiority is not clearly defined you must be satisfied with attacking in a moderate pace, advancing on your strong points and methodically creating new ones near your opponent's lines of defence. Then the *plan* is everything, and the time a matter of secondary importance (compare the 3rd, 4th, 5th and 6th game given in these lectures). Generally the "pace" of your attack must slacken down, the less pronounced your advantage is. A very good player will seldom give you opportunities for violent and short attacks, which require an amount of acting force that is often underrated.

Some of Morphy's games:

Game #13
Schulten vs. Morphy
New York, 1857
King's Gambit

1.	e4	e5
2.	f4	exf4
3.	Bc4	d5
4.	exd5	Nf6

5.	Nc3	Bd6
6.	d4	0-0
7.	Nge2	f3

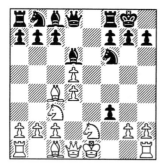

Occupying one of White's *strong points*, that can be attacked only by the f-pawn or the queen bishop, therefore an excellent obstruction.

10.	....	Bg3†
11.	Kd2	Bd6
12.	Kc3	....

Here he unnecessarily exposes himself to new dangers. 12. c3 would have provided a safe retreat to the king.

| 12. | .... | b5 |

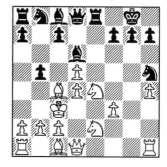

Quickly opening up all the lines on the side which the white king has chosen to take refuge.

| 13. | Bxb5 | c6 |

Now he threatens 14...Qa5†, so he indirectly forces White to remove the well posted knight from e4.

14.	Nxd6	Qxd6
15.	Ba4	Ba6
16.	Re1	Nd7 [17]
17.	b3	Nb6
18.	Bxc6	Rac8 [18]

Every one of Black's pieces has now long open lines in consequence of the energetic attacking manoeuvres of the last six moves.

The white king stands in an obstructed file, so Morphy sacrifices his pawn to prevent the king from castling with safety. It will be remarked that after the sacrifice, the defensive power of the white h- and f-pawns becomes very weak, both of these pawns being isolated.

| 8. | gxf3 | Nh5 |
| 9. | h4 | .... |

It would have been better to defend by a developing move such as 9. Be3, when the following play might ensue: 9...Re8 10. Qd2 Qe7 11. Ne4 Bf5 12. Bd3.

| 9. | .... | Re8 |
| 10. | Ne4 | .... |

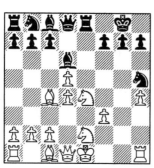

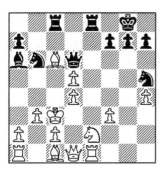

■ 19. **19.** Kd2 [19] ....

Black threatened to win a piece by knight or queen takes d5. 19. Kb2 would have lost immediately on account of 19...Rxc6 20. dxc6 Bxe2 21. Rxe2 [20] Rxe2 22. Qxe2 Na4† either winning the queen or checkmating the king in the next move.

19.	....	Rxc6 [21]
20.	dxc6	Bxe2
21.	Rxe2 [22]	Qxd4†
22.	Ke1	Qg1†
23.	Kd2	Rd8†
24.	Kc3	Qc5†
25.	Kb2	Na4†

0-1

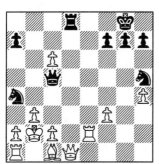

Resigns, for if 26. bxa4 Qb4 mate. If 26. Kb1 Nc3† winning first the queen and then the rook.

His famous game against Paulsen in the New York Tournament runs as follows.

Game #14
Paulsen vs. Morphy
New York, 1857
Four Knights Game

1.	e4	e5
2.	Nf3	Nc6
3.	Nc3	Nf6
4.	Bb5	Bc5
5.	0-0	0-0
6.	Nxe5	Re8

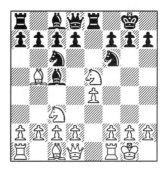

| 7. | Nxc6 | .... |

This capture only develops Black. it would have been quite as good to retire 7.Nf3 and to follow this up, if 7...Nxe4, by 8. d4.

7.	....	dxc6
8.	Bc4	b5
9.	Be2	....

The black pawns by thus advancing do not of course gain in defensive strength, but Black is so far ahead in development that White will never be able to take advantage of that weakness.

9.	....	Nxe4
10.	Nxe4	Rxe4
11.	Bf3	....

If here 11. c3, which looks at first sight stronger, then Black will assail the castled king, which for the present has only the support of the h- and g-pawns. The game might proceed 11...Qh4 12. g3 Qh3 13. Bf3 Rh4 14. gxh4 Bd6 or 12. d4 Bd6 13. g3 Qh3 14. f4 Bd7 15. Bf3 Re7

Analysis: after 15...Re7

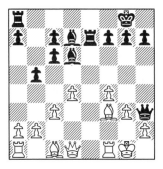

when Black will double his rooks on the e-file and obtain a sound position with many attacking possibilities.

| 11. | .... | Re6 |
| 12. | c3 | .... |

A somewhat elaborate process for so simple an object. First, 12. d3 was the proper play.

| 12 | .... | Qd3 |

This is one of the rare cases in which a heavy piece like the queen can with success be used for the purpose of ob-

struction. The queen cannot be attacked in her present situation by any hostile man but exerts a considerable amount of pressure, preventing, for instance, such moves as Qc2 or Be2.

♦ 13.	b4	Bb6
14.	a4	bxa4
15.	Qxa4	Bd7
16.	Ra2	....

This move may serve as a preparation for Qc2. White evidently is beginning to feel the restraint which he suffers through the blockade of his queen pawn by the adverse queen. His plan, however, is frustrated by Black, whose attack has already become ripe for the decisive blow.

If 16. Qa6 (instead of 16. Ra2), Black's best reply seems to be 16...Qf5 17. d4 Rae8 18. Be3 c5 19. bxc5 Bxc5

Analysis: after 19...Bxc5

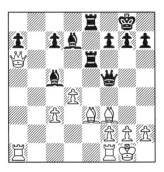

20. Qa5? Rg6 with a winning advantage. For if 21. Kh1 Qxf3 22. gxf3 Bc6 leaves White helpless.

Therefore White's best would be 20. Qe2 Bb6 21. Bg4 Rxe3 22. Bxf5 Rxe2 23. Bxd7 with an even ending.

| 16. | .... | Rae8 |

The strongest move for development and simultaneously for attack. Black threatens now 17...Qxf1†.

| 17. | Qa6 | Qxf3 |

An effective, surprising, and beautiful coup.

| 18. | gxf3 | Rg6† |
| 19. | Kh1 | Bh3 |

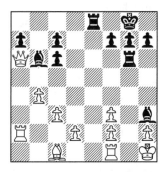

Black threatens 20...Bg2† followed by 21...Bxf3 mate. 20. Rg1 is no safeguard, as after the exchange of the rooks, the queen rook will checkmate him. Nor would 20. Qd3 mend matters, as Black will answer with 20...f5, and if then 21. Qc4† by 21...Kf8.

20.	Rd1	Bg2†
21.	Kg1	Bxf3†
22.	Kf1	Bg2†

He might have decided the issue by

22...Rg2 with the double threat of 23...Rxf2† and 23...Rxh2.

| 23. | Kg1 | Bh3† [23] |
| 24. | Kh1 | Bxf2 |

| 25. | Qf1 | .... |

His only resource.

| 25. | .... | Bxf1 |
| 26. | Rxf1 | Re2 |

Again binding the hostile d-pawn to his post.

| 27. | Ra1 | Rh6 |
| 28. | d4 | .... |

At last!

| 28. | .... | Be3 |
| | 0-1 | |

Resigns, for if 29. Bxe3 Rhxh2† 30. Kg1 Reg2 checkmate.

Let us now pass over to more recent times.

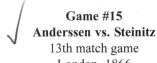

Game #15
Anderssen vs. Steinitz
13th match game
London, 1866
Ruy Lopez

1.	e4	e5
2.	Nf3	Nc6
3.	Bb5	Nf6
4.	d3	d6
5.	Bxc6†	....

This exchange is decidedly uncalled for. Black's queen rook gains thereby an open line as well as the queen bishop. White has no compensation whatever; for to speak in the early stages of a game of the weakness of a doubled pawn, or an isolated pawn, for end game purposes is nothing but a chimera.

5.	....	bxc6
6.	h3	g6

Black has already the advantage and can therefore afford to lose a move for development, which will later on support his plan of attack.

7.	Nc3	Bg7
8.	0-0	0-0

9.	Bg5	h6
10.	Be3	c5

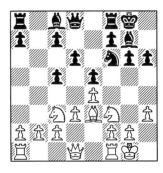

An excellent coup. Black's plan as will be seen is to make the fighting on the kingside with his pawns. He therefore keeps the white d-pawn back to preserve the obstructions in the centre.

11.	Rb1	....

It would have been much more to White's interest to forestall the imminent attack, for instance, by 11. Qd2 Kh7 12. g4 Ng8 13. Nh2 f5 14. f3.

11.	....	Ne8
12.	b4	cxb4
13.	Rxb4	c5
14.	Ra4	Bd7
15.	Ra3	f5

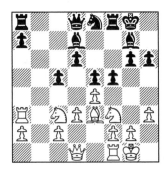

The white e-pawn, which intercepts the line of the bishop from c6, blocks the e5-pawn, and holds back the d6-pawn, dare not be removed. It is, therefore, an excellent object of attack.

16.	Qb1	Kh8
17.	Qb7	a5
18.	Rb1	a4
19.	Qd5	Qc8

White's game suffers from want of design. There is no possible object in all this manoeuvering of the heavy pieces. His policy should have been one of defence, which he might conduct by 19. Nh2, 20. f3 and so on, and perhaps successfully.

20.	Rb6	Ra7

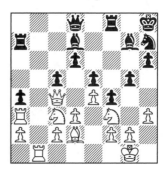

In order to have his queen free for the following threat: 21...f4 22. Bd2 Bxh3 23. gxh3 Qxh3 24. Nh2 f3 etc.

21.	Kh2	f4
22.	Bd2	g5
23.	Qc4	Qd8
24.	Rb1	Nf6
25.	Kg1	Nh7

The h-pawn shall advance and then the g-pawn, to be followed by ...Ng5, where the knight will have in conjunction with his advanced pawns, a commanding sway. Mark how carefully all this is prepared. No strong point is left to the white party in the rear of the black

pawns, nor in front of them, during the whole of the tedious process.

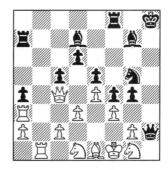

26.	Kf1	h5
27.	Ng1	g4
28.	hxg4	hxg4
29.	f3	Qh4
30.	Nd1	Ng5
31.	Be1	Qh2

Here we have the *beau ideal* of the concluding stages of a kingside attack supported by a chain of pawns. If 32. fxg4, all the lines are opened by 32...f3 with tremendous effect. White cannot much improve his position as his pieces have no space to execute any movements. So Black has any amount of time to prepare the finishing stroke.

32.	d4	gxf3
33.	gxf3	Nh3
34.	Bf2	Nxg1
35.	dxc5	....

Of course if 35. Bxg1 Bh3† wins.

| 35. | .... | Qh3† |
| 36. | Ke1 | .... |

or 36. Kxg1 Bf6, the white king being quite helpless.

| 36. | .... | Nxf3† |
| 37. | Rxf3 | Qxf3 |

and Black won easily a few moves later...

38.	Nc3	dxc5
39.	Bxc5	Rc7
40.	Nd5	Rxc5
41.	Qxc5	Qxe4†
42.	Kf2	Rc8
43.	Nc7	Qe3†

0-1

Do not overlook how the apparently unimportant sixth move of White (h3)

was the real reason of all the trouble that he had to undergo later.

Game #16
Steinitz vs. Zukertort
2nd match game
New York, 1886
Scotch Game

1.	e4	e5
2.	Nf3	Nc6
3.	d4	exd4
4.	Nxd4	Nf6

According to our rules this should be the strongest reply. It certainly is a move that answers all purposes.

5.	Nc3	Bb4
6.	Nxc6	bxc6
7.	Bd3	d5
8.	exd5	cxd5
9.	0-0	0-0
10.	Bg5	c6
11.	Ne2	Bd6

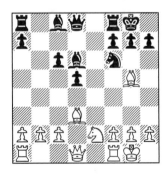

| 12. | Ng3 | .... |

The knight occupies a square which is better reserved for the bishop. 12. Nd4 seems therefore preferable.

| 12. | .... | h6 |
| 13. | Bd2 | Ng4 |

Excellent! Black threatens ...Qh4. If White replies by 14. h3, then 14...Nxf2 15. Kxf2 Qh4 15. Qf3 f5 winning.

14.	Be2	Qh4
15.	Bxg4	Bxg4
16.	Qc1	....

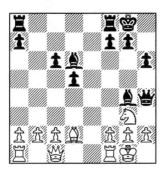

| 16. | .... | Be2 |

What he proposes with this is not very clear. He ought to strike hard while White is yet behind in the development of his rooks, thus: 16...f5 17. Bf4 Bc5 18. Re1 g5 19. Be3 Bxe3 20. fxe3 f4 with an excellent attack. Or even 16...Bd7 will give him a lasting attack, difficult to meet.

17.	Re1	Ba6
18.	Bc3	f5
19.	Re6	Rad8
20.	Qd2	....

Now he threatens Qd4, or the doubling of rooks on the open file; but mark how finely Black frustrates all this.

| 20. | .... | d4 |
| 21. | Ba5 | .... |

Of course he cannot take the pawn without losing a piece.

21.	....	Rd7
22.	Rxd6	Rxd6
23.	Bb4	Qf6
24.	Rd1	Rd5
25.	Bxf8	Qxf8
26.	Nh5	Qe8
27.	Nf4	Re5

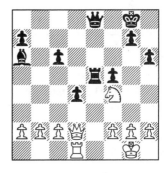

Black is the first to take the open file—a great advantage, which White should not have yielded at move 26.

| 28. | h4 | c5 |
| 29. | h5 | .... |

This manoeuvre with the h-pawn, which shall make the position of the N unassailable, is misplaced. The pawn

55

exposes itself only to the attack of the bishop.

| 29. | .... | Re4 |
| 30. | c3 | .... |

This unnecessary advance is the principle reason for the speedy conclusion that follows. Black's play from now to the end is admirably consistent and strong.

30.	....	Qb8
31.	g3	Qe5
32.	Ng6	Qd6
33.	Nf4	d3

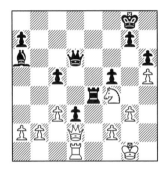

| 34. | b3 | .... |

If 34. Nxd3 Bxd3 35. Qxd3 Re1† wins the rook or the queen.

34.	....	c4
35.	Rb1	Kh7
36.	Kh2	Qb6

First rate; he now threatens 37...Re2.

37.	Kg1	Bb7
38.	Rb2	Qc6
39.	f3	Qc5†
40.	Qf2	Re1†
41.	Kh2	....

or 41. Kg2 Re3.

| 41. | .... | Qxf2† |
| 42. | Rxf2 | Bxf3 |

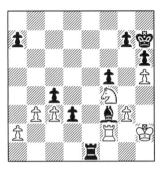

Decisive. The d-pawn must now win.

43.	g4	Be2
44.	Ng2	d2
45.	Ne3	cxb3
46.	axb3	Bxg4

0-1

If we glance critically over the games given, we find two rules confirmed:

(1) Don't attack unless you have some tangible superiority, either in the stronger working of your pieces, or in longer reach. Corollary: If you do, the reaction will place your army in a critical position, and the inevitable counter attack will find you in disorder.

(2) Let it be the first object of your attack to create strong points as near your opponent's camp as possible, and oc-

cupy them with pieces which have from there a large field of action.)
Corollary: Try to force your opponent's pawns to advance on the side where you attack.

Game #17
Dr. Noa vs. Dr. Tarrasch
Dresden, 1892
Ruy Lopez

1.	e4	e5
2.	Nf3	Nc6
3.	Bb5	Nf6
4.	0-0	Nxe4
5.	Re1	Nd6
6.	Ba4	Be7
7.	Nxe5	Nxe5
8.	Rxe5	0-0

Now Black's development is excellent and the pawn position unassailable.

9.	d4	Nc4
10.	Re1	d5

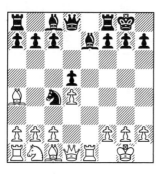

11.	c3	....

White has no time for such a move. 11. Bb3 Na5 12. Nc3 Nxb3 13. axb3 Bd6 14. Qf3 c6 15. Bf4 is a sounder line of play.

11.	....	Bf5

Immediately bearing down on the weak points of White, d3 and c2.

12.	Nd2	Nxd2
13.	Bxd2	Bd6
14.	Qh5	....

This manoeuvre has not much point. 14. Bc2 is more to the purpose.

14.	....	Bg6
15.	Qh3	c6

From here to the end Black's play is simply classical. Mark now how finely Black will combine the advantage resulting from the weak position of the white queen, the slight weakness contained in the loose, ineffective positions of the white bishops, and his own strongly posted queen bishop, and the lack of protection of the white b-pawn, for a highly logical and successful attack.

16.	Re2	Qb6
17.	Bb3	a5

Capital! Developing the QR, dislodging the obstruction, and keeping the b-pawn in its unsafe position.

18.	Be3	a4
19.	Bd1	Rfe8
20.	Rc1	f5

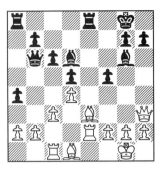

Grand! He forces White to advance either the g- or f- pawn. In the latter case e4 becomes a very strong point, in the former, the queen is obstructed and the pawn position weakened.

21.	f4	Re7
22.	R1c2	Rae8
23.	Bc1	Qb5

Preventing Qd3 and again bearing down on the central weak points of the White game.

24.	Qf3	Qc4
25.	a3	Re4
26.	g3	c5

To get his reserve force, the king bishop, into play.

27.	Rxe4	fxe4
28.	Qe3	Qd3
29.	Qxd3	exd3
30.	Rf2	b5
31.	Bd2	Be7
32.	f5	Bf7
33.	Rf1	cxd4
34.	cxd4	Bf6
35.	Bc3	Re4
36.	Bf3	Bxd4†
37.	Kg2	....

A mistake. 37. Bxd4 Rxd4 38. Rd1 is by far the preferable policy.

| 37. | .... | Bxc3 |

Energetic and decisive, but not very difficult to foresee.

38.	Bxe4	dxe4
39.	bxc3	Bb3
	0-1	

and White resigns, for after 40. Kf2 d2 41. Ke2 Bc4† he will lose his rook.

One of my match games.

Game #18
Lasker vs. Blackburne
10th match game
London, 1892
Queen's Gambit Declined

1.	d4	d5
2.	Nf3	Nf6
3.	c4	e6
4.	Nc3	Nbd7

5.	Bf4	c6

On account of the last move which is more or less forced (not to allow Nb5) the development chosen by Black is not advisable.

6.	e3	Nh5
7.	Bg5	Be7
8.	Bxe7	Qxe7
9.	Bd3	g6
10.	Qe2	0-0
11.	0-0	f5

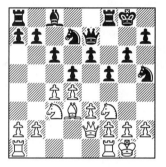

Attacks on the kingside in this opening have usually little hope of success. An inspection of the position shows that the K-side does not present weakness that could be assailed. The fight is therefore in the centre and on the queenside.

12.	Rfd1	Ndf6
13.	Rac1	Bd7
14.	Ne5	Be8
15.	Qc2	....

With his 11th move Black has stopped the advance of the white e-pawn. The white queen is therefore available for the Q's wing.

15.	....	Rd8
16.	a3	Nd7
17.	Nf3	Ng7

18.	Re1	....

White intends a queenside attack; and, therefore makes first preparations to take advantage of any forward movement that Black might undertake on the kingside, beginning with f5-f4.

18.	....	Nf6
19.	b4	Ne4
20.	Ne5	Nxc3
21.	Qxc3	Nh5
22.	a4	Nf6
23.	b5	Nd7
24.	Nf3	....

White threatens now 25. c5, followed by a4-a5-a6, to establish a dangerous passed pawn at c5.

24.	....	dxc4
25.	Qxc4	Nb6
26.	Qb3	cxb5
27.	axb5	Bf7
28.	Ne5	Rc8
29.	Ra1	....

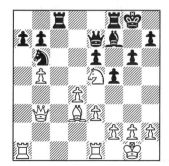

The object of White's attack was to keep the queen rook pawn back, which is now indefensible.

29.	....	Ra8
30.	Re2	Rfc8
31.	R2a2	Qc7
32.	g3	Qc3
33.	Qxc3	Rxc3
34.	Rxa7	Rxa7
35.	Rxa7	Rc7

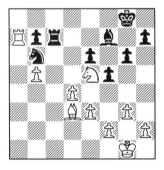

The attack has succeeded. White has the advantage of a pawn plus on the kingside. What remains is to convert this into positional superiority—not any easy process, as still there are hardly any assailable points in the black camp.

36.	Kf1	Be8
37.	Ke2	Kf8
38.	Kd2	Ke7
39.	Ra3	Kd6
40.	f3	Rc8
41.	e4	Rc7
42.	Ra1	Rc8
43.	h4	Rc7
44.	Rb1	Rc8
45.	Ke3	Ke7
46.	h5	....

The decisive manoeuvre. If the pawn is taken, the two isolated h-pawns will be a splendid object of attack, well worth the sacrifice.

46.	....	Kf6
47.	hxg6	hxg6
48.	Rh1	Kg7

Here, after some manoeuvres to complete the third hour (we played eighteen moves an hour) the game went on at move 55, the position being unchanged.

49.	Ra1	Ra8
50.	Rc1	Rc8
51.	Rb1	Kf6
52.	Rh1	Kg7
53.	Ra1	Ra8
54.	Rh1	Rc8
55.	g4	fxg4
56.	fxg4	Ra8
57.	g5	....

Threatening Ng4-f6. And so on.

57.	....	Ra3
58.	Kd2	Ra2†

59.	Ke3	Ra3
60.	Kf4	Nd7
61.	Bc4	Nf8
62.	Rc1	....

The finishing stroke. The rook will now enter via c7 into the black camp.

62.	....	Ra5
63.	Bd3	Bxb5
64.	Rc5	Ra4
65.	Bxb5	Rxd4
66.	Rc7†	Kg8
67.	Rxb7	

1-0

Chapter Eight

The Defence

Gentlemen:

The principles of defence will be the subject of our lecture tonight. If the attack is the process through which obstructions are brought out of the way, the defence is the art of strengthening them, of giving firmness to your position, and of averting the blow directed against you. When your position is not inferior to that of your opponent, and he nevertheless makes preparations to attack you, disregard them altogether, develop reserve forces, avoid his attack by the slightest defensive movement possible (like a first-rate boxer, who in the nick of time and with an almost imperceptible movement evades the blow), and institute a quick counter action.

When you, however, have been unfortunate enough to compromise yourself, to give your opponent an undeniable reason for and tangible object of attack (which may occur to the best and most cautious player as the result of an unsuccessful attack), you have to act very differently.

Also here common sense tells us exactly how to proceed. Every position will comprise points which are exposed to the action of the hostile forces and other points which are well guarded. An attack will direct itself in the first instance against your weakest points—for instance, against the h- and g-pawn after castling. Or against a knight on f3/f6, etc.

You will therefore, first of all, evacuate these points if they are occupied by men of great importance, the queen or rook, for instance, and also frequently a knight and a bishop. Secondly, you will have to give them support; place the support in points which are not easily accessible by the enemy. The rest of your army is best employed in engaging the reserve force of the enemy—that is, such force which it will take him time and labor to utilize for the purposes of his attack.

The object of your opponent's attack is generally speaking, to change the position of your men in a certain quarter by force. Abstain from changing it voluntarily, except for the most forcible reasons.

This is where most Chess players fail. In order for instance to avoid the approach of a knight or bishop to g5/g4, they advance their h-pawns to h3/h6, losing a move and besides, as a general rule, impairing the defensive strength of the chain of pawns on the wing.

Or they advance the g-pawn to g3/g6, to drive a knight away posted on f5/f4, which however well placed, is usually not half as dangerous as this move itself. Or they retire a piece because it may be driven away.

Wait with all such moves until your antagonist has expended some time, material, position, etc.,—well, call it taken altogether, some of the "power" at his disposal—on them.

For the rest your defensive movements must of course be subservient to the objects of the enemy's attack. You may therefore reverse the rules for attack. Let it be your object to prevent your opponent from creating strong points very near your line of defence. That comprises everything, as we shall see in the instances that are to follow.

Game #19
Delmar vs. Lipschütz
New York, 1888
Scotch Game

1.	e4	e5
2.	Nf3	Nc6
3.	d4	exd4
4.	Nxd4	Nf6
5.	Nxc6	bxc6
6.	Bd3	d5
7.	e5	....

Black has followed up to this point the rules of development. He has given White no object of attack nor are any of his pieces in a weak position. White's attacking manoeuvre is therefore premature.

7.	....	Ng4
8.	0-0	Bc5
9.	h3	....

Now follows a clever stroke which

shows how unsound all White's play has been.

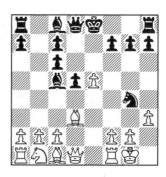

9.	....	Nxe5
10.	Re1	Qf6
11.	Qe2	0-0
12.	Qxe5	Qxf2†
13.	Kh1	Bxh3
14.	gxh3	Qf3†
15.	Kh2	Bd6
16.	Qxd6	Qf2†

0-1

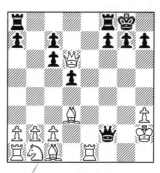

Game #20
White vs. Black
Max Lange Attack

1.	e4	e5
2.	Nf3	Nc6
3.	d4	exd4
4.	Bc4	Bc5
5.	0-0	Nf6

5...d6 would be more in conformity with our rules. The text move is slightly inferior and gives White the opportunity to initiate a violent onslaught, which, however, in the face of Black's splendid development, fails against the best line of defence.

6. e5 ....

6. .... d5

The right reply. To remove the knight would be vastly inferior. If 6...Ne4 then 7. Bd5 would disorganize Black's game, and if 6...Ng4 7. Bxf7† Kxf7 8. Ng5† might follow.

7.	exf6	dxc4
8.	Re1†	Be6
9.	Ng5	....

9. .... Qd5

Not 9...Qd7 as 10. Nxe6 fxe6 11. Qh5† would allow White to gain the king bishop.

| 10. | Nc3 | Qf5 |
| 11. | g4 | Qg6 |

Black must not take 11...Qxf6 as White would answer 12. Nd5 Qd8 13. Rxe6† fxe6 14. Nxe6. Now Black threatens to castle queenside with a magnificent game, as White, through his attacking manoeuvres, has vastly impaired the solidity of his position.

12.	Nce4	Bb6
13.	f4	0-0-0
14.	f5	Bxf5
15.	gxf5	Qxf5

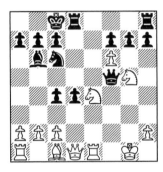

At last White has recouped himself in material, but at what an expense! He is three pawns behind, his king is in a totally unsafe position, his enemy is brilliantly developed. In addition the d- and c-pawns, far advanced and well protected, are ready for decisive action whenever the slightest opportunity is offered. All this for a minor piece.

16.	fxg7	Rhe8 [24]
17.	Ng3	d3†
18.	Be3	Bxe3†
19.	Rxe3	Qc5

Or 19...Qxg5 winning. Similar conclusions follow in any variations that White may choose after move 13.

Therefore let us go back to that position and vary the attack.

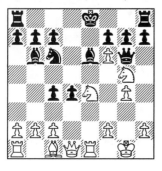

13.   Nxf7   ....

A bold sacrifice to maintain the attack. If king or queen takes knight, 14. Ng5 will regain the piece with an excellent position. If 13...Bxf7 White must be satisfied with driving the king into a somewhat exposed position by 14. fxg7 Qxg7 15. Nf6† Kd8 16. Qf3, with good attacking possibilities against the exposed king.

Black, however, has just as bold a reply, which utterly turns the tables, and gives him the attack against the weakened K-side of White.

13.   0-0

Now at once, all the white pieces become badly placed and must speedily

return to their camp. The tide turns and the reaction sets in.

14.	Nfg5	Bd5
15.	fxg7	Rfe8
16.	Ng3	h6
17.	Nh3	Ne5

And Black should win. Or perhaps more effectively...

17.	.. ..	Rxe1†
18.	Qxe1	Re8
19.	Qd1	Ne5
20.	Nf4	Qc6

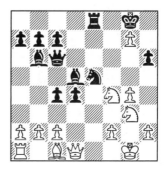

With a brilliant attack.

Game #21
N.N. vs. Rutherford
Liverpool, 1800s
Ponziani Opening

1.	e4	e5
2.	Nf3	Nc6
3.	c3	....

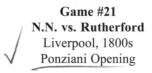

The Ponziani Opening. I cannot recommend it to you on account of the questionable early advance of the c-pawn which it involves.

| 3. | .... | d5 |

An excellent answer. By his third move White has weakened the square d3, so Black tries to open the d-file to get possession of that very important point.

4.	Qa4	dxe4
5.	Nxe5	Qd5
6.	Bb5	Nge7
7.	f4	....

This is the move given by Staunton. It is intended to keep up the attack which by the exchange of minor pieces would be utterly lost. White threatens now 8. Bc4 and Staunton lets Black, therefore, reply by 7...exf3. A fine Liverpool player, looking at the position with the instinct of a true chess player, thought that there must be, against such a precipitate attack as White has undertaken, a better reply. And this is how he defeated one of his opponents in a match game.

7.	....	Bd7
8.	Nxd7	Kxd7
9.	0-0	Nf5

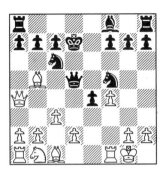

Black has by far the better development and now threatens 10...Bc5†.

10.	b4	a5
11.	Kh1	axb4
12.	Bxc6†	bxc6
13.	Qxa8	Bc5

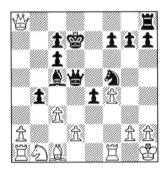

14.	Qxh8	Ng3†
15.	hxg3	Qh5#
	0-1	

Checkmate.

Game #22
Blackburne vs. Burn
Bradford, 1888
French Defence

1.	e4	e6
2.	d4	d5
3.	Nc3	Nf6
4.	e5	Nfd7
5.	f4	c5

6.	dxc5	Bxc5
7.	Qg4	0-0
8.	Bd3	f5
9.	Qh3	Nc6
10.	Nf3	Re8

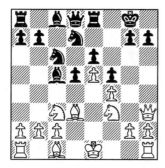

Black is evidently preparing his K-side for a long siege. His last move answers that purpose excellently. The rook vacates the square f8 for the knight, which is there quite secure, and gives support to the weakest point, the h7-pawn; besides to e6 and g6, and is always ready to obstruct the g-file.

11.	g4	g6
12.	a3	....

One of those harmless looking moves, to prevent something that really is no threat at all. These superfluous defensive moves spoil many a game. Why not at once 12. Qg3, and then a vigorous advance of the h-pawn?

12.	....	a6
13.	Bd2	b5
14.	gxf5	gxf5
15.	0-0-0	Nf8
16.	Rhg1†	....

A bold and promising sacrifice which yields a violent attack, difficult to meet.

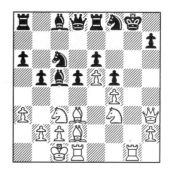

16.	....	Bxg1
17.	Rxg1†	Ng6
18.	Ne2	Ra7

Again an excellent defensive manoeuvre. The rook protects several of the weakest points and can be used as a means of obstructing the open g-file.

19.	Ng3	Ree7
20.	Nh5	Kh8
21.	Nf6	Rg7
22.	Qh6	Nf8
23.	Ng5	....

Black is practically out of danger but must yet play very carefully. White intends now to continue with 24. Qxg7† Rxg7 25. Nf7† Rxf7 26. Rg8 mate.

23.	....	Rg6
24.	Qh5	R7g7
25.	Rg3	Qe7

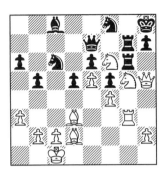

Another protection to the h7-pawn. White's attack slackens down because his two bishops cannot find an outlet to add their weight to it.

| 26. | Be2 [25] | Rxf6 |

Vigorous and decisive.

27.	exf6	Qxf6
28.	Rc3	Bd7
29.	Nf3	Kg8

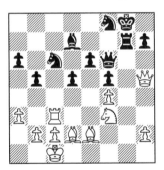

White threatened 30. Rxc6 followed by 31. Bc3.

30.	Qh3	Ng6
31.	Qh6	Qe7
32.	Rxc6	....

A last attempt to neutralize Black's material superiority by attack.

| 32. | .... | Bxc6 |

33.	Bc3	Rf7
34.	Ng5	Nxf4
35.	Nxf7	Nxe2†
36.	Kd2	Nxc3

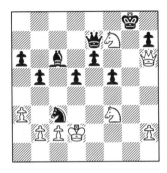

and Black won after a few more moves.

Game #23
Lasker vs. Steinitz
3rd match game
New York, 1894
Ruy Lopez

1.	e4	e5
2.	Nf3	Nc6
3.	Bb5	d6
4.	d4	Bd7
5.	Nc3	Nge7
6.	Bc4	exd4
7.	Nxd4	Nxd4
8.	Qxd4	Nc6
9.	Qe3	Ne5
10.	Bb3	Be6

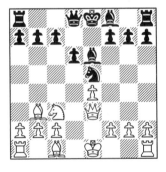

| 11. | f4 | Nc4 |

12.	Qg3	Nb6
13.	Be3	c6
14.	f5	Bxb3
15.	axb3	Nd7
16.	Bf4	Qc7
17.	b4	f6
18.	Ne2	Ne5

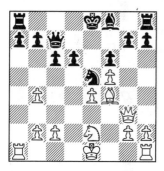

19.	Nd4	Qb6
20.	c3	0-0-0
21.	Ne6	Rd7
22.	Be3	Qb5
23.	Rxa7	b6
24.	Ra8†	Kb7
25.	Rxf8	Rxf8
26.	Nxf8	Qd3

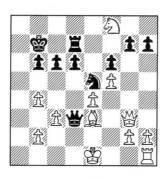

The annexed position occurred in my match with Mr. Steinitz; White to move. I played somewhat hastily

27.	Rf1	....

being under the impression that 27.

Nxd7 leads to a draw by perpetual check. However, this is not the case as pointed out by Tchigorin, e.g. 27. Nxd7 Qb1† 28. Kd2 Qxb2† 29. Kd1 Qb3† 30. Ke2 Qc4† 31. Ke1! Qxc3† 32. Bd2 Qa1† 33. Ke2, and White should easily win.

27.	....	Qc2
28.	Bd2	Re7
29.	Ne6	Qxe4†

Here White must be extremely careful in selecting his reply. If he plays the plausible 30. Kd1 Qb1† 31. Bc1 Nd3 32. Qxd6 Nxb2† 33. Ke2 Qe4† 34. Be3[26] Qxe3† equalizing the material forces, with good chances for a draw.

30.	Qe3	Qxg2

Now follows a very important manoeuvre, the key to White's defence.

31.	b3	....

If 31. Qe2 instead, Black will answer by 31...Qd5 and have all the queenside at his own disposal.

31.	....	Re8

To take the h2-pawn would not be sufficient to keep the balance of forces. White would reply 32. Kd1 or 32. b5,

69

and very soon be able to assume the attack.

| 32. | Qe2 | Qh3 |

The first symptom of the gradual exhaustion of Black's attack. The queen would be better posted somewhere on the queenside. But 32...Qd5 is not playable as 33. c4 forces the exchange of queens.

| 33. | Kd1 | Ra8 |
| 34. | Rf2 | Ra2 |

Black's pieces are well placed, but they do not threaten anything.

35.	b5	c5
36.	Nxg7	d5
37.	Kc1	....

White threatens to drive the rook away, in order to bring matters speedily to a climax.

| 37. | .... | Qd3 |

37...c4 is answered by 38. bxc4; 37...Nd3† by 38. Kb1. The resulting exchanges leave White always in the possession of his advantage.

38.	Qxd3	Nxd3†
39.	Kb1	Rb2†
40.	Ka1	Rxb3
41.	Rf3	....

And White won the ending:

41.	.. ..	c4
42.	Ne8	Nb4
43.	Rg3	Ra3†
44.	Kb1	Rb3†
45.	Kc1	Nd3†
46.	Rxd3	cxb3
47.	Nxf6	Rxb5
48.	Ne8	Kc6
49.	f6	d4
50.	Ng7	dxc3
51.	Bxc3	Rg5
52.	f7	

1-0

Game #24
Steinitz vs. Lasker
18th match game
Montreal, 1894
Queen's Gambit Declined

| 1. | d4 | d5 |
| 2. | c4 | e6 |

3.	Nc3	Nf6
4.	Bg5	Be7
5.	Nf3	0-0
6.	e3	Nbd7
7.	Rc1	c6
8.	Bd3	dxc4
9.	Bxc4	Nd5
10.	Bxe7	Qxe7

25.	Rc2	f5
26.	exf5	exf5
27.	Qf2	g6
28.	Nf4	Ncd7
29.	Nd5	Qd6
30.	Rcd2	Rc1
31.	Ne3	Rxd1
32.	Nxd1	Qe6

11.	e4	Nf4
12.	g3	Ng6
13.	0-0	Rd8
14.	Qe2	b5
15.	Bb3	Bb7
16.	Qe3	a6
17.	Ne2	Rac8
18.	Rfd1	Re8
19.	Ne1	c5
20.	dxc5	Nxc5
21.	Bc2	Rc7

This diagram shows the state of my game No. 18, at move 33, White to play, of my match with Mr. Steinitz. I recommend to you the careful study of this position, in which White can keep the balance only by a very ingenious manoeuvre of defence. The question concerns *only* the next move of White. Black threatens 33...Nxf3† 34. Nxf3 Bxf3 35. Qxf3 Qe1† winning.

How is White to save his game?

If 33. Rc2 Rxc2 34. Bxc2 Qc6 35. Kg2 Nxf3 36. Nxf3 Ne5 will regain the piece and keep the pawn plus.

If 33. Re2 Rc1 34. Bc2 Qd5 35. Ne3 Qxf3, or else 35. Rd2 Nxf3† 36. Nxf3 Qxf3 37. Qxf3 Bxf3 38. Rxd7 Rxc2 should win.

22.	f3	R8c8
23.	Bb1	Ne5
24.	b3	f6

33. Ne3 may be answered by 33...Rc1 34. Rd1 Nxf3† 35. Nxf3 Rxd1† 36. Nxd1 Qd5 again remaining a pawn ahead, with at least an even position.

If 33. Kg2 Nxf3 34. Nxf3 Ne5 35. Rd3 Rc1 36. Rd8† Kg7 37. Qa7 Qc6 will yield an irresistible attack to the second player.

The move actually made, and the only one to save the game (which ended in a draw) was ...

33.   Kf1!   ....

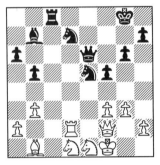

against which Black must play very cautiously not to be at a disadvantage. Any too violent attack will fail.

33.	.. ..	Rc5
34.	Qe3	Rd5
35.	Rxd5	Qxd5
36.	Nc3	Qc6
37.	Kf2	Kg7
38.	Ne2	Qd6
39.	Nd4	Qf6
40.	Ng2	Nc6 [27]

41.	Ne6†	Kg8
42.	Bc2	Qe5 [28]
43.	Ngf4	Qxe3†
44.	Kxe3	Nb4
45.	Bb1	Ne5
46.	Nd4	Kf7
47.	a3	Nd5†
48.	Nxd5	Bxd5
49.	Bd3	Ke7
50.	Be2	Kd6
51.	f4	Nd7

52.	g4	fxg4
53.	Bxg4	Nb6
54.	h4	Bb7
55.	Be6	Nd5†
56.	Bxd5	Kxd5
57.	Nf3	Bc8
58.	Ng5	h5
59.	Ne4	Bf5
60.	Nc3†	Kc5
61.	Ne4†	Kd5

½-½

Sometimes you will have to look very deeply into the position to find a good move for the defence. But this much I believe I can promise you, that if you follow the rules laid down, you will not search in vain. If you will seek, you will find, no matter how dangerous the attack may look.

Chapter Nine

The End Game

Gentlemen:

When both parties through the struggles of the middle game have held their own, when by the exertions undergone in attack and defence, the material forces on both sides have become decimated, and direct attacks on the king have consequently lost any chance of success, the game enters upon a new stage, differing in many points from those preceding it.

Of this part of the game, called the end game, it is a characteristic that the king—hitherto the direct or indirect object of attack on the part of your opponent—over whose safety you anxiously watched, and whose power was limited to protection of a few pawns needed for his own security, now becomes a powerful weapon of offence and aggression in your hands.

When the game enters this last stage, the general rules for attack and defence are not changed in any particular. Weaknesses will principally be represented by pawns which are blocked or cannot advance for some other reason, and which besides, cannot be defended by other pawns. Here again the attack will direct itself against the weaknesses. Our weak points will be such as are open to the enemy's men, and not commanded by any of our own men; our opponent's forces will be directed towards those strong points, and will attempt to create new ones as near the hostile weaknesses as it has the power to do. Here also the attacking party needs for success a superiority of some kind. But in combination with all this two new factors enter into the end game which give it its peculiar character.

The first is based on the greater facility acquired (in consequence of the exhaustion of the material forces) to lead your passed pawns to queen. For that purpose there are never more than five separate moves required and often less. If the line where the pawn advances consists entirely of strong points, the enemy will obliged to engage one of his men, perhaps his king, whose function it will be to command one of these points or to obstruct that line.

Points and lines through which the hostile men prevent the advance of the passed pawn may be called *points of vantage* in regard to it. The game will very often then present a fight for command of these points or lines of advance, which may be intercepted by our men, or from which the hostile forces may be driven back. On the other hand, being quite satisfied with the result that part of the hostile army is engaged in watching our passed pawn, we may undertake an attack with all our forces in some other quarter.

When attack and defence in the very latest stages of the game are so evenly balanced, and both our own men and those of the opponent are so favorably placed, that, unless the adversary voluntarily gives way, neither party can improve his position, when, in other words, the move ceases to be a privilege, "time" (the right to move, that is to do something useful), will assume a new and very different aspect.

In such positions as are frequent in well contested games, and the occurrence of which can often with certainty be forecalculated, to have to move means often a *loss* in the working power of your pieces, and it may consequently lose you the game. We shall speak of this as the *principle of exhaustion*, (that is, exhaustion of moves to *improve* your position). This principle will manifest itself in the great care with which the two combatants hold back certain moves, which either would improve their position or at least not affect it harmfully, until a favorable opportunity has arrived for executing them.

The principle of exhaustion may be illustrated by the diagrams.

White, manoeuvering on the h- or g-file, has no chance to force the win. There is not sufficient space at his disposal. For instance, after 1. Kh3 Kh6 2. Kh4 Kg6, he would have to recede. Therefore we must leave that quarter of the board to the black king. Our h-pawn will consequently be a weakness and it will be wise to hold it back as long as possible.

The best position for the black king to occupy will be g4. Whenever he will

occupy that square our king must be ready to march to e3 or e5. From this we deduce the following line of play...

1.	Kh3	Kh6
2.	Kg2	Kh5
3.	Kg3	Kh6

The first manifestation of the principle.

| 4. | Kf2 | Kh5 |

| 5. | Ke2 | .... |

Not 5. Ke3, as 5...Kg4 would win a pawn.

5.	....	Kh4
6.	Kd3	Kg4
7.	Ke3	Kh3
8.	Kd4	Kxh2
9.	Ke5	winning

In this position,

White has two chances of winning, one based on his passed pawn, the other on the weakness of the a6-pawn. The black king occupies at present a position of advantage in regard to both. This is changed by the following manoeuvre:

1.	Kd5	Kc8
2.	Kc4	Kd8
3.	Kd4	Kc8
4.	Kd5	Kc7
5.	Kc5	...

Now the move is changed, and White wins easily, or

4.	....	Kd8
5.	Kd6	Kc8
6.	c7	Kb7
7.	Kd7	....

And mates in a few more moves.

An ending by Mr. Locock.

White has two dangerous attacks; the one against the weak black g-pawn, the king threatening it from f4; the object of the other is to advance his pawn to e5, supported by the K at d4.

Therefore when the white king will be at e3, the black king must be able to occupy in that moment g5. And when the white king stands on d4 the black king must prevent the threatened advance by marching to f6. If then the white king is at d3, ready to go in one move to either of these squares (d4/e3), the hostile king must stand on g6.

Thus the different squares on each side correspond to each other. This mode of reasoning followed up, we come to the conclusion that White with the move draws, Black with the move loses.

For example, if Black moves first,

1.	....	Kh8
2.	Kb2	Kg8
3.	Kb3	Kh7
4.	Kc2	Kh6
5.	Kd2	Kh5
6.	Kc3	Kg5
7.	Kc4	Kg6
8.	Kd3	Kg5
9.	Ke3	winning

Or

8.	...	Kf6
9.	Kd4	Kg6
10.	e5	dxe5†
11.	Kxe5	Kf7
12.	Kf5	winning

Now let White have the move.

1.	Kc2	Kh7
2.	Kd2	Kh6
3.	Ke2	Kh5
4.	Kd2	Kh6

5.	Kc2	Kh7
6.	Kc3	Kg7
7.	Kc4	Kf7

8.	Kd4	Kf6
9.	Kd3	Kg6
10.	Ke3	Kg5 etc.

One of the gentlemen present, Mr. McLaren, asked for an explanation of the following position [a study by H. Neustadtl published in 1890]:

This position depends also on the principle of exhaustion. Black's points of advantage, from which he attacks the white pawn are three—e2, e3, f4. The most forward and therefore best of these is e2. Whenever the black king is there, the white king must be ready to occupy g2. And whenever the black king marches to e3, the white king must take the point g3. The game will run therefore...

76

1.	Kh1	Kd2
2.	Kh2	Kd3
3.	Kh3	Kd4
4.	Kg4	Ke3

5.	Kg3	Ke2
6.	Kg2	Kd1
7.	Kh1	....

(Or 7. Kh3[29]) and draws.

An attempt to force one of the passed pawns will fail.

1.	Kh1	g4
2.	Kg2	....

And draws.

Black with the move will win:

1.	....	Ke1
2.	Kg2	Ke2
3.	Kg3	Kf1
4.	Kh3	Kf2

5.	Kg4	Kg2

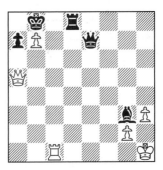

Winning.

The following positions are illustrative of the power of the passed pawn.

White wins by a clever stroke, in which all the powers of the b7-pawn are made use of.

1.	Rc8†	Rxc8
2.	Qxa7†	Kxa7
3.	bxc8=N†	....

Wins the queen and the game.

The above is more of a mid game combination than an end game type, but even backed by very little force, a passed pawn can be very dangerous.

1.	Nf3	Bd8
2.	Ne5	Kh7
3.	Ng4	Kh8
4.	Nf6	

And wins, as Black has to move; if 3...Bh4 4. Nf6† would obstruct the bishop's diagonal and therefore win.

1.	Bd4	Bg3
2.	Ba7	Bf4
3.	Bb8	Be3
4.	Bc7	Ba7
5.	Bb6	....

And wins in a few more moves. In both of the latter cases the king of the winning party is exceedingly well placed.

The difference in the position of the kings decides the struggle.

1.	Kb8	Rb2†
2.	Ka8	Rc2
3.	Rf6†	Ka5

If 3...Kb5 4. Kb8 would speedily win.

4.	Kb8	Rb2†
5.	Ka7	Rc2
6.	Rf5†	Ka4

7.	Kb7	Rb2†

78

8.	Ka6	Rc2
9.	Rf4†	Ka3
10.	Kb6	Rb2†
11.	Ka5	Rc2
12.	Rf3†	Ka2
13.	Rxf2!	

And wins by queen against rook.

Black to Play

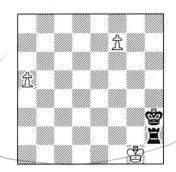

1.	....	Rg2†
2.	Kf1	Rg4
3.	f8=R	....

If pawn queens instead, 3...Rf4† sacrificing itself, would force the stalemate.

3.	....	Ra4
4.	Ra8	Kg4

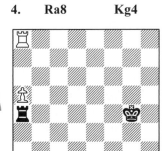

An excellent move. White threatened 5. a6, 6. a7, and then a check with his rook. If now 5. a6 Kf3 threatening mate, will force the draw, for instance 6. Ke1 Ke3 7. Kd1 Kd3 8. Kc1 Kc3 9. Kb1 Rb4† and so on.

5.	Ke2	Kf5
6.	a6	Kf6

Not 6...Ke6 as 7. a7 Kd7 8. Rh8 would gain the rook.

7.	Kd3	....

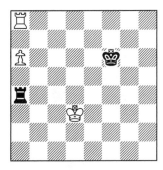

The decisive manoeuvre. The king comes to the support of the pawn, in order to liberate the rook, while Black can do nothing to change the position to his advantage. The square a7 is left free for the king, to allow him a place of safety against the checks of the black rook.

7.	....	Kg7
8.	Kc3	Kh7
9.	Kb3	Ra5
10.	Kb4	Ra1
11.	Kb5	Rb1†
12.	Kc6	Rc1†
13.	Kb7	Rb1†
14.	Ka7	....

Without this place of refuge the game would never be won. Now it is a very simple matter.

14.	....	Kg7
15.	Rb8	Ra1
16.	Rb6	Kf7
17.	Kb7	....

Winning easily.

Here White wins by his superior king position and because his pawns are further advanced than those of Black.

1.	Kf4	... ..

It is necessary to time the winning manoeuvre correctly. Therefore we must not at once march to e4.

1.	....	Kf8
2.	Ke4	c5
3.	Kd3	Ke8
4.	e7	....

The right moment for the advance. Now Black's movements are forced.

4.	....	Kd7
5.	Kc4	Ke8
6.	Kxc5	d3
7.	Kd6	d2
8.	Ke6	d1=Q
9.	f7#	

1-0

Checkmate.

| 1. | a5 | Bh6 |

The a-pawn has only to pass one more dark square and that within two moves; therefore the bishop must hurry to stop it.

| 2. | g5† | Bxg5 |

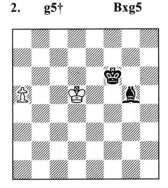

The bishop is obstructed by his own king.

| 3. | Ke4 | Bh4 |
| 4. | Kf3 | .... |

And the pawn will queen.

When the end game stage is nearing, the power of the various pieces is altered to a marked degree. Different issues being at stake, different measures must be adopted, and ideas, correct in the earlier part of the game, become sensibly modified. The value of each piece varies of course with each end game position in a greater or lesser degree; but the men have a certain average value which will serve as a guide. This value will be determined—

(a) By their fighting capacity against the adverse king as an aggressive piece,
(b) and against passed pawns,
(c) and finally their *reach* or power of offence, when obstructions (as is usual in endgames) are few.

Let us first consider the king. Being well placed in opposition to the adverse king, he will take three squares from him, and can thus hinder him from advancing.

He can, single-handed, stop three united passed pawns, not advanced beyond the sixth row; and two, one of which is on the seventh row. He can attack every square on the board and that, if he is in a central point, for instance at e4, in no more than three moves.

His reach is totally uninfluenced by obstructions other than the natural limits of the board. He is therefore, a powerful weapon, if well developed in one of the central points or near important points.

He can, however, never be used as an instrument of obstruction, never be exposed to any direct attack, which sensibly diminishes his offensive value against strong pieces of offence.

Game #25
Harrwitz vs. Morphy
5th match game
Paris, 1858
Dutch Defence

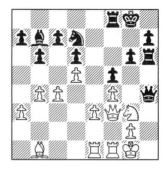

1.	d4	f5
2.	c4	e6
3.	Nc3	Nf6
4.	Bg5	Be7
5.	e3	0-0
6.	Bd3	b6
7.	Nge2	Bb7
8.	0-0	Nh5
9.	Bxe7	Qxe7

10.	Ng3	Nxg3
11.	hxg3	d6
12.	f4	Nc6
13.	g4	Nb4
14.	gxf5	exf5
15.	Qd2	Rae8
16.	Rae1	Qh4
17.	Bb1	Re6
18.	Qf2	Qh5
19.	d5	Rh6
20.	Qf3	Qh4
21.	a3	Na6
22.	b4	Nb8
23.	Ne2	Nd7
24.	Ng3	g6

25.	Kf2	Nf6
26.	Rh1	Ng4†
27.	Kg1	Qf6
28.	Rxh6	Nxh6
29.	Qd1	Ng4
30.	Qd2	Qh4
31.	Nf1	Re8
32.	g3	Qh3
33.	b5	Nf6
34.	Qg2	Qxg2†
35.	Kxg2	

The annexed position occurred in one of Morphy's match games. The game went on...

35.	....	a6
36.	a4	axb5
37.	axb5	Ra8

The first advantage, an unopposed open file for the rook is now established.

38.	Nd2	Ra3

39.	e4	fxe4
40.	Nxe4	Nxe4
41.	Bxe4	Rc3
42.	Bf3	....

Threatening now, of course, 43. Re8†
and 44. Rb8.

42.	....	Kf7
43.	Re4	Bc8
44.	Be2	Bf5
45.	Rd4	h5

Through this last move the important
point at f5 becomes strong.

46.	Kf2	Kf6
47.	Rd2	Bc2
48.	Ke1	Be4
49.	Kf2	Kf5

The white king is kept back by the black
rook. The black king, however, can advance unchecked.

50.	Ra2	h4

Forcing the way for his king which soon
becomes a dangerous assailant.

51.	gxh4	Kxf4
52.	Ra7	Rh3
53.	Rxc7	Rh2†
54.	Ke1	Ke3

0-1

Crushing every resistance.

Game #26
Lasker vs. Steinitz
9th match game
Philadelphia, 1894
Ruy Lopez

1.	e4	e5
2.	Nf3	Nc6
3.	Bb5	d6
4.	Nc3	a6
5.	Bc4	Be6
6.	Bxe6	fxe6

7.	d4	exd4
8.	Nxd4	Nxd4
9.	Qxd4	Ne7
10.	Bg5	Nc6
11.	Bxd8	Nxd4
12.	0-0-0	Nb5
13.	Nxb5	axb5
14.	Bxc7	Rxa2
15.	Bb6	Be7
16.	c3	Kf7
17.	Kc2	Rha8
18.	Kb3	R2a4
19.	f3	R8a6
20.	Bd4	g6
21.	Rd3	Ke8

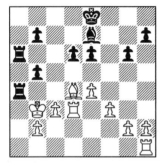

In one of my match games with Mr. Steinitz the above position occurred, with White to move.

22.	Rhd1	e5

If 22...Kd7 at once, 23. f4 will give White a good game.

23.	Be3	Kd7
24.	Bc5	Ra1
25.	R1d2	Ke6
26.	Ba3	g5
27.	Rd5	Rb6
28.	Kb4	....

Now the king actively enters the fight.

28.	....	g4

The initiation of a subtle counter attack which nearly succeeds in turning the tables.

29.	Ka5	....

It might have been wiser first to accept the offered pawn thus: 29. fxg4 Re1 30. Ka5 Bd8 31. Rxb5 Ra6† 32. Kb4 Rxe4† 12. Kb3, remaining a pawn ahead.

29.	....	Ra6†
30.	Kxb5	h5

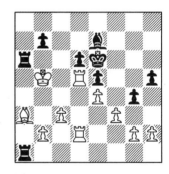

Or 30...Rh1 31. fxg4 Re1 32. h3 Rxe4 33. c4.

31.	Rd1	Rxd1
32.	Rxd1	gxf3
33.	gxf3	Ra8
34.	Kb6	Rg8
35.	Kxb7	Rg2
36.	h4	Rh2

84

37.	Kc6	....

This manoeuvre makes the black game untenable.

37.	....	Bxh4
38.	Rxd6†	Kf7
39.	Kd5	....

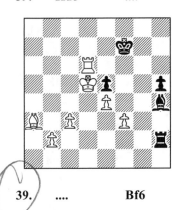

39.	....	Bf6

If 39...Rd2† 40. Kxe5 Bg3† 41. f4 Rxd6 42. Bxd6 h4 43. Bc5 h3 44. Bg1 and the four passed pawns win easily against the bishop.

40.	Rd7†	Kg6
41.	Ke6	....

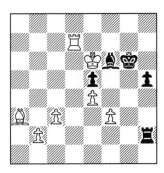

To check the advance of the black king. If now 41...Kg5 42. Rf7 Bd8 43. Rf8 Bb6 44. Be7† Kg6 45. Rg8† Kh7 46. Kf7 followed by Bf6 would draw the black king into a mating net.

41.	....	h4
42.	Rd1	h3
43.	Rg1†	Rg2
44.	Rxg2†	hxg2
45.	Bc5	....

And wins after a few more moves with his passed pawns.

45.	....	Bd8
46.	b4	Kg5
47.	Kd7	Bf6
48.	b5	Kf4
49.	b6	

1-0

Another of Morphy's energetic end game attacks.

Game #27
Morphy vs. Salmon
One of eight blindfold
Birmingham, 1858
Evans Gambit

1.	e4	e5
2.	Nf3	Nc6
3.	Bc4	Bc5
4.	b4	d5
5.	exd5	Nxb4
6.	0-0	Ne7
7.	Nxe5	0-0
8.	d4	Bd6
9.	Nc3	Bf5
10.	Bb3	a5
11.	a3	a4

12.	Nxa4	Nbxd5
13.	c4	Rxa4
14.	cxd5	Ra5
15.	Qf3	Bg6

16.	Re1	Bb4
17.	Re2	Nf5
18.	Bb2	Qa8
19.	g3	Qa7
20.	Nxg6	hxg6
21.	Re5	Bxa3
22.	d6	Bb4
23.	Rexa5	Bxa5
24.	Qd5	b6
25.	d7	Qa8
26.	Rc1	Qxd5
27.	Bxd5	b5

28.	Bc6	Nd6
29.	d5	Bd2
30.	Rd1	Bg5
31.	f4	Bd8
32.	Ba3	f5
33.	Re1	Kf7
34.	Bxb5	Rh8

35.	Bxd6	cxd6

36.	Re8	Rf8
37.	Kf2	g5
38.	Ke3	g4
39.	Kd3	g5
40.	Bc6	gxf4
41.	gxf4	Rg8
42.	Kc4	....

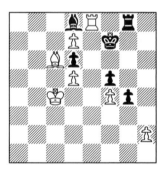

The black forces being all engaged by the combined action of the white rook, passed pawn, and bishop, the cooperation of the king is all that is necessary to decide the day.

42.	....	Rf8
43.	Kb5	Rg8
44.	Ka6	Rf8
45.	Kb7	Rg8
46.	Kc8	Bb6
47.	Rxg8	Kxg8
48.	d8=Q†	Bxd8
49.	Kxd8	

1-0

Examples concerning the power of the king could be readily multiplied. But we leave this for a future occasion. The king as an assailant, or as a strong protective power, being an essential element, yea, almost an organic part of each approximately even end game.

Another piece whose power increases the more the end game stage is approaching is the rook. His fighting capacity against the adverse king is enormous, and exactly what makes him a valuable instrument for attack as well as defence.

In conjunction with his own king he can checkmate the hostile king driven to the edge of the board. And in combination with a knight and pawn and a single obstruction he can give checkmate to a king on any square of the board. An example:

Without any kind of support he can give untold checks to the adverse king, until the same is obliged to approach the rook, perhaps against the best interests of his game, or forced to protect himself behind some kind of obstruction. On account of his attacking qualities he is always a valuable ally when you want to force any obstructions out of the way, for instance, of passed pawns.

But he is less fit for fighting against them. And really too valuable a piece to be given away for such a purpose, if other alternatives are open. The best way to stop an adverse passed pawn with a rook is to place the rook behind it, as his reach will increase the more the pawn advances.

He can stop, and even win (if they are unsupported) two passed pawns, of which one is on the sixth, the other on the fifth row. But two passed pawns on the sixth row will queen against him if united.

Used against advanced pawns he is therefore not as manageable as the king or even the bishop. But he is more dangerous to the pawns before they assume a threatening attitude, as his reach is very great, and exactly calculated to serve against pawns in their strongest position—that is, when they are abreast.

He can attack, if unobstructed, any square of the board in one move, and will command fourteen at a time. This enables him to restrict the opposite king to a portion of the board.

The bishop is very much less fit for assault against the king, or for restricting his approach, than the rook. The bishop can take away two squares from the king, and eventually give check and command two squares of the reach of the king. His capacity for yielding support to passed pawns is not very great as the line in which the pawn advances will usually contain some points where obstructions are totally safe against him. His great value consists in two things:

(1) That he can stop adverse pawns from a long distance and from a number of squares.

(2) That a pawn and a bishop may protect each other, so as to make both of them comparatively safe against the king or superior pieces.

His chessboard, however, contains only thirty-two squares, and whichever influence they may have on the issue of the game, very much determines his share in it; so that his importance may be exaggerated when you have the superiority of position, or almost annihilated when the opposite is the case.

The knight is, unless circumstances are very favorable, the weakest piece of all. He may take two squares from the king, or give check, and besides take away one square from him. But the adverse king may approach him then and get rid of him if no more support is near.

His great power is that he cannot be obstructed. When obstructions abound, and when he can often occupy a strong point near the enemy's line, he can be an invaluable ally. His reach never exceeds eight points, situated in a circle. And he may be obliged to take five moves to cross the board from one point to another (for instance, the two diagonally opposite corner points). On an extended field of battle he must therefore choose the wing to which he will give his support, or very much lose in value.

To refer to the oft mooted question, "Which piece is stronger, the bishop or the knight?" it is clear that the value of the bishop undergoes greater changes than that of the knight. If experience

has shown that, on an average, during the opening or middle game, the bishop will be at least as strong as the knight, this will be the more true the more obstructions disappear, that is, in endings with only a few pawns scattered about the board. In complicated end game positions, where pawns partly form blocks, the knight will find his best chance.

The value of two bishops varies, of course, as they dominate the whole chess board, very much less than that of one; in consequence, two bishops are as a rule appreciably stronger than two knights or a bishop and a knight.

From a correspondence game.

| 1. | Ne4 | b5 |
| 2. | a3 | .... |

Now all the dark squares on the queenside are in possession of White; nor can this be changed as the black king is necessary on the kingside to fight against the white pawns.

2.	....	Bg6
3.	f3	Kf7
4.	Kf2	Ke6
5.	Ke3	h6
6.	g4	Kd5
7.	Nc3†	Kd6

| 8. | f4 | Be8 |

It would have been more advisable to keep the bishop in the rear of the advancing pawns.

| 9. | f5 | Bd7 |
| 10. | Ne4† | .... |

| 10. | .... | Ke7 |

If 10...Kd5 11. f6 will force the exchange of knight for bishop and the extra pawn will easily win.

11.	Kf4	Be8
12.	Ke5	Bf7
13.	h4	Bd5
14.	g5	hxg5
15.	hxg5	Bg8
16.	g6	

1-0

Black resigns as f5-f6 will soon prove decisive.

From another game by correspondence. Black to move.

| 1. | .... | c5 |

Strong and embarrassing to White. The pawn engages the d4-pawn which is the only white unit that commands the point e5. It can therefore, not take the hostile pawn, as after 2. dxc5† bxc5, White has no means to stop the check at e5, which would soon prove fatal to him.

| 2. | Rh7 | .... |

Unsatisfactory enough, but the knight cannot move to any square improving his position, and without exposing the white pawns to the attack of the rook.

2.	....	cxd4
3.	exd4	Nf4†
4.	Kc3	Ne6

Now White can do nothing effectual. If the rook moves Black will win the d4-pawn, 5...Nxd4 6. Kxd4 Rxd2†.

| 5. | Kd3 | a5 |
| 6. | Ke3 | Rg1 |

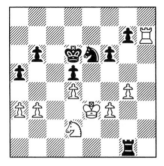

This manoeuvre with the rook is splendid. He threatens now 7...Rc1 and 8...Rc3†, winning the d-pawn. White cannot frustrate that plan, *e.g.* 7. Kd3 Rc1 8. a4 Nf4† 9. Ke3 g5 11. Kf2 Rd1etc.

7.	Rh8	Rc1
8.	Rb8	Rc3†
9.	Kf2	Nxd4
10.	Rxb6†	Ke5
11.	Rb7	Kf4

If now 12. Rxg7 Rc2 13. Ke1 Ke3 14. Re7† Kd3 15. Nf1 Nxf3† 16. Kd1 d4, and White has no satisfactory move left.

| 12. | g5 | Re3 |
| | **0-1** | |

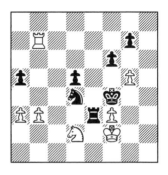

And White resigns, for after 13. gxf6 gxf6 14. Rf7 f5, his position becomes altogether untenable.

Game #28
Schlechter vs. Tchigorin
Hastings Rd. 21, 1895
Ruy Lopez

1.	e4	e5
2.	Nf3	Nc6
3.	Bb5	a6
4.	Ba4	Nf6
5.	0-0	d6
6.	d4	Nd7
7.	Nc3	Be7
8.	Ne2	0-0
9.	c3	Bf6
10.	Ng3	Ne7
11.	Bb3	Ng6
12.	Be3	Re8

| 13. | Qd2 | Ndf8 |
| 14. | dxe5 | dxe5 |

15.	Qxd8	Bxd8
16.	Ng5	Bxg5
17.	Bxg5	Be6
18.	Ne2	Bxb3
19.	axb3	Ne6
20.	Be3	Rad8
21.	Rfd1	f6
22.	f3	Kf7
23.	Kf2	Ke7
24.	g3	Ngf8
25.	Ke1	Nd7
26.	Nc1	g5
27.	Nd3	h5
28.	Ke2	Rh8

It was White's turn to move and the game went on

29.	b4	....

A pawn move without a clearly defined purpose is to be blamed. The pawn at b4 takes away a good square from the knight, which that piece ought to have occupied at once in order to threaten 30. Nd5† and to force the advance 29...c6, which would greatly increase the strength of the bishop. Moreover, it leaves a strong point at c4 to the black knights, which White can only guard by another advance of a pawn (b2-b3).

29.	....	Rdg8
30.	Rg1	....

He ought not to leave the important d-file with his rook. All defensive purposes could be served just as well by 30. h3, which would enable him to reply to 30...g4 with 31. fxg4 hxg4 32. h4, and to 30...h4 with 31. g4.

30.	....	g4
31.	f4	Nd8
32.	f5	Nf7
33.	Nf2	Nd6
34.	Bc5	....

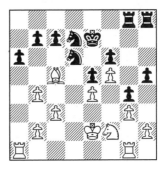

34.	....	Nb6

Not 34...Nxc5, as 35. bxc5 N-moves 36. c6 would follow.

35.	Nd1	....

Now decidedly 35. Rd1 was the right place, when for instance 35...Rd8 36. Rxd6 Rxd6 37. Rd1 would lead to a probable draw.

35.	....	Nbc8
36.	Ne3	Kf7

Now the e4-pawn has become indefensible.

37.	Nd5	c6
38.	Nc7	Nxe4
39.	Rad1	Nxc5
40.	bxc5	Rd8

41.	Ne6	Rxd1
42.	Rxd1	Ke7

43.	h4	....

In thus opening up files for the black rook he plays Black's game. 43. c4 is by far preferable. Neither the black knight nor the rook will then ever be to obtain good positions. 43...h4 could then be answered by 44. gxh4 Rxh4 45. Rd8 Na7 46. Ra8 winning the piece.

43.	....	gxh3
44.	Rh1	Kf7
45.	Rxh3	Ne7
46.	g4	h4
47.	c4	Ng6

A pretty little move which threatens 48...Nf8.

48.	fxg6†	Kxe6
49.	g7	Rg8
50.	Rxh4	Rxg7

51.	Ke3	Kf7

It remains to force the exchange of the last pawn on the kingside, in order to have there all lines free, and a clear superiority.

52.	b4	....

52.	....	Kg6

If the plausible 52...Kg8 instead, then 53. Ke4 Rh7 54. Rxh7 Kxh7 55. Kf5 Kg7 56. g5 fxg5 57. Kxg5, drawing without difficulty.

53.	Rh8	f5
54.	gxf5†	Kxf5

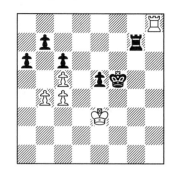

55.	Rh5†	....

55. Rf8† would find its reply in 55...Ke6 56. Re8† Kd7 57. Rxe5 Rg3† 58. K-moves Rb3 when Black will remain with a winning advantage.

55.	....	Ke6
56.	Rh6†	Kd7
57.	b5	axb5
58.	cxb5	cxb5
59.	Ke4	Re7
60.	Rb6	Kc7
61.	Rxb5	Kc6
• 62.	Ra5	Re8

68.	Rc1†	Kd7
69.	Rc5	Kd6
70.	Rb5	Kc6
72.	Rb1	b5
73.	Rc1†	Kb6
74.	Rb1	Re8
• 75.	Rb2	Kc5
76.	Rc2†	Kb4
77.	Rb2†	Kc4

0-1

This manoeuvre with the rook, which wins a move, decides the game. The white king dare not move as otherwise the black e-pawn advances still further; so all White's moves are forced.

And White resigned the struggle which Black had masterfully conducted.

THE END

63.	Ra7	Re6
64.	Ra5	Re7
65.	Ra1	Kxc5
66.	Rc1†	Kd6
67.	Rd1†	Kc6

This brings to a close the original version of *Common Sense In Chess*. The two chapters following contain additional Lasker material from the period, and were added by the editor.

Chapter Ten

Last Round at Hastings

Your editor was curious. How did Schlechter-Tchigorin work its way into *Common Sense?* It was played in early September 1895, so it was not part of the lecture series given in the spring. Mechanically it was easy enough to do, work up the manuscript and add the game at the end, which is what Lasker did. But what sparked his interest in the first place?

A check in the tournament book shows that it was annotated by Steinitz, so it was not one of six games Lasker had contracted to comment upon. Then it hit me. It was the last round.

To get our bearings let's look at the scores going into the final round:

    1. Pillsbury 15½
    2. Tchigorin 15
    3. Lasker 14½

Tarrasch and Steinitz had 12 and were out of the running for one of the top three prizes. This meant that even if Lasker lost he had third place locked up.

Now the pairings:

    Pillsbury-Gunsberg
    Schlechter-Tchigorin
    Burn-Lasker

Mathematically Lasker still had a chance to tie for first, if Pillsbury lost and if Tchigorin lost or drew. Of course Lasker had to win and score 15½ to have any chance at all. If Pillsbury won

or drew there was still a shot at second place, clear if Tchigorin lost, but only tied if he drew.

Here's how it looked to the editor of the tournament book: "The three leaders all had dangerous opponents of the first rank. As the day goes on the first two leaders seemed likely to draw, whilst Lasker has made a brilliant sacrifice which wins."

So Lasker did what he had to do, beating Burn in twenty moves. That meant waiting around for the other two games to finish. Pillsbury-Gunsberg was eventually decided in Pillsbury's favor at move forty, a classic ending that has made its way into countless anthologies.

So first place was out. What about second? Schlechter-Tchigorin was adjourned. For much of the game Schlechter looked to be holding his own. Lasker's hopes were high until Schlechter weakened and dropped a pawn. But even afterwards there were still good drawing chances since White's pieces were active and Black's were not. Could Schlechter hang on and salvage the draw?

The game seemed to go on forever and we can only imagine how Lasker must have suffered as he watched it unfold.

As we know Tchigorin played the ending magnificently, notching up the full point, nosing Lasker out for second. And as we also know now this was merely the first occasion where Schlechter made Lasker suffer, the other main occasion being their 1910 world title match.

So now we can understand what sparked Lasker's interest in this particular game. Let's look at the other two from the final round.

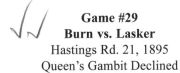

Game #29
Burn vs. Lasker
Hastings Rd. 21, 1895
Queen's Gambit Declined

Notes by Pillsbury in the book of the tournament.

1.	d4	d5
2.	c4	e6
3.	Nf3	Nf6
4.	Nc3	c5

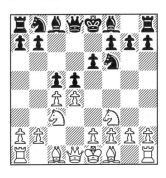

| 5. | e3 | .... |

In a game between Blackburne and Showalter the former here continued with 5. Bg5. *(A prophetic note. Four months later at St. Petersburg, Pillsbury played 5. Bg5 against Lasker, a memorable encounter, brilliantly won by Lasker. BA.)*

5.	....	Nc6
6.	cxd5	exd5

7.	Bd3	a6
8.	dxc5	Bxc5
9.	0-0	0-0
10.	Bd2	Re8
11.	Rc1	Ba7

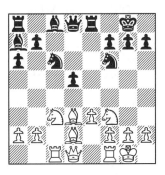

| 12. | Ne2 | .... |

It would be better to prevent the pinning by 12. h3; Black has much the freer position of pieces, fully compensating for the isolated pawn.

12.	....	Bg4
13.	Bc3	....

13. Ng3 at once was the correct move, and would have prevented the formation of the attack which ensues.

13.	....	Ne4
14.	Ng3	Nxf2

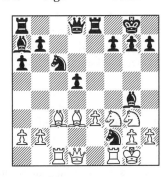

This pretty sacrifice leads to fine complications, but there appears to be a flaw in it.

95

| 15. | Rxf2 | Rxe3 |
| 16. | Nf5 | .... |

Why not simply Be2? If in answer 16...Qb6 then 17. Nd4 or if 16...Bxf3 17. Bxf3 Qb6 18. Qf1. White appears to retain at least the exchange ahead in all variations.

| 16. | .... | Rxf3 |

Black now demolishes the opposing position with a few well-chosen, timely strokes.

17.	gxf3	Bxf5
18.	Bxf5	Qg5†
19.	Bg4	h5
20.	Qd2	Be3
	0-1	

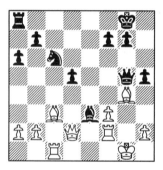

Game #30
Pillsbury vs. Gunsberg
Hastings Rd. 21, 1895
Queen's Gambit Declined

1.	d4	d5
2.	c4	c6
3.	e3	g6
4.	Nc3	Bg7

Black chooses a peculiar but not altogether sound manner of development. The objection to this mode of bringing out the bishop is that it costs two moves,

brings the bishop on a line which is blocked, and allows the first player possibilities of a kingside attack beginning with h4.

5.	Nf3	Nf6
6.	Bd3	0-0
7.	Ne5	dxc4
8.	Bxc4	Nd5
9.	f4	Be6
10.	Qb3	....

So far White has treated the opening to perfection. But here 10. Bd3 soon followed by h4 seems preferable.

10.	....	b5
11.	Bxd5	Bxd5
12.	Nxd5	Qxd5
13.	Qxd5	cxd5

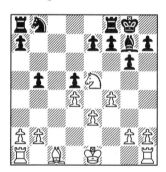

| 14. | Nd3 | .... |

He must now try to reserve his knight for the ending as the abundance of obstructions leaves little scope to the bishops and rooks.

14.	....	Nd7
15.	Bd2	Rfc8
16.	Ke2	e6
17.	Rhc1	Bf8
18.	Rxc8	Rxc8
19.	Rc1	Rxc1
20.	Bxc1	Bd6

21.	Bd2	Kf8
22.	Bb4	Ke7
23.	Bc5	

| 23. | .... | a6 |

Almost obviously 23...a5 would have been better and would have reduced White's chance to win to zero. For instance: 23...a5 24. b4 axb4 25. Bxb4 Bxb4 26. Nxb4 Kd6 27. g4 f6 soon followed by ...e5.

| 24. | b4 | f6 |
| 25. | g4 | Bxc5 |

And here 25...Nxc5 26. bxc5 Bc7 would have left the game perfectly even, a bishop being so much more suitable to stop advancing pawns.

| 26. | bxc5 | Nb8 |

His best continuation was 26...a5 when the following play would have been

possible: 27. f5 g5 28. c6 Nb6 29. Nc5 exf5 30. gxf5 Kd6 31. Nb7† Kxc6 32. Nxa5† Kc7 and Black has, if anything, the better chances, as he threatens ...Nc4 and ...Nd6.

| 27. | f5 | .... |

White's play from here unto the end is of the highest order. If this pawn is taken, 27...gxf5 28. gxf5 exf5 then 29. Nf4 follows, which would ensure to White the advantage of two united passed centre pawns. If on the other hand 27...exf5 28. gxf5 g5 29. Nb4 would lead to the same result.

27.	....	g5
28.	Nb4	a5
29.	c6	....

Threatening of course c7.

| 29. | .... | Kd6 |
| 30. | fxe6 | .... |

If now 30...axb4 then 31. e7 Kxe7 32. c7.

30.	....	Nxc6
31.	Nxc6	Kxc6
32.	e4	....

The key to this remarkable combination. Whether the offered pawn is taken

or not White will always win with his
two united passed pawns, *e.g.* 32...Kd6
33. exd5 Ke7 34. Ke3 Kd6 35. Ke4 Ke7
36. Kf5 b4 37. d6† and wins.

32.	....	dxe4
33.	d5†	Kd6
34.	Ke3	b4

34...f5 would finds its reply in 35. gxf5
b4 36. f6 a4 37. f7 Ke7 38. d6† Kf8
39. d7 Ke7 40. f8=Q† etc.

35.	Kxe4	a4
36.	Kd4	h5
37.	gxh5	a3
38.	Kc4	f5
39.	h6	f4
40.	h7	

1-0

Chapter Eleven

Lasker Annotates

Lasker contracted to annotate six games for the Hastings 1895 tournament book. Pillsbury-Gunsberg appears in Chapter Ten. Here are the others.

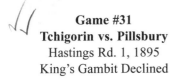

Game #31
Tchigorin vs. Pillsbury
Hastings Rd. 1, 1895
King's Gambit Declined

1.	e4	e5
2.	f4	Bc5
3.	Nf3	d6
4.	Bc4	Nc6
5.	Nc3	Nf6
6.	d3	Bg4
7.	h3	Bxf3

An early exchange of bishop for knight being as a rule objectionable, some of the best players prefer to remove this bishop to e6, relying on the speedy development of their pieces, which in their opinion, forms a compensation for the doubled pawn (after Bxe6 fxe6).

8.	Qxf3	Nd4
9.	Qg3	....

To remove queen to d1 is hardly advisable. Although there might be no vital objection against it, yet it would seem that after 9. Qd1 Nd7 Black will obtain a free and open game with many good chances, for no sacrifice in material or position whatever.

9.	....	Nxc2†
10.	Kd1	Nxa1
11.	Qxg7	....

11.	....	Kd7

The only possible move in this position as proved by "book" long ago. The reply to 11...Rf8, for instance, might be 12. fxe5 dxe5 13. Rf1 Be7 14. Bg5 Nh5 15. Bxf7† Kd7 16. Qxe5 when obviously Black's game must fall to pieces.

12.	fxe5	dxe5
13.	Rf1	Be7

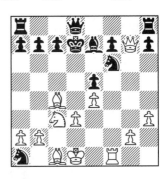

14.	Qxf7	....

Although Mr. Tchigorin must have had his reasons why he should prefer this capture to the apparently stronger and more natural continuation 14. Bg5, we fail to see what Black could have replied to such an attack. To corroborate our opinion we give the following variations: *[What follows is an intricate analysis, one of the longest notes Lasker ever wrote. We'll save it for the end.]*

14.	....	Kc8
15.	Bg5	Rf8
16.	Qe6†	Kb8
17.	Bh6	Re8
18.	Qxe5	Nd7
19.	Qh5	....

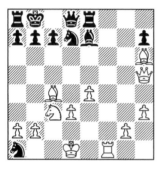

19.	....	Nb6

So far Black's defensive manoeuvres have been perfect. Although he is a rook ahead, the strong position of all the white men and pawns, the blocked positions of the king and queen rook, and finally, the exposure of the knight at a1, place it beyond doubt that White must be in the advantage. Black ought, therefore, not to disdain a possible draw.

His best course seems to be 19...Bf8 20. Bg5 Be7 21. Bh6 Bf8 22. Be3 Bg7 23. Kd2 Ne5 or 23. Qxh7 Bxc3 24. bxc3 Ne5 [or Nf6] when Black has a great many chances for a successful counter-attack.

The move actually made makes it impossible for him to bring his rook at e8 speedily into play as now 20...Bf8

would be answered by 21. Qxe8 Qxe8 22. Rxf8 etc.

20.	Bd5	a6
21.	Kd2	Nxd5
22.	Nxd5	Rg8
23.	g4	....

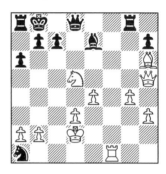

23.	....	Bb4†

An ingenious manoeuvre whose outcome is that the bishop is exchanged for the knight. Pretty though it is, it appears doubtful whether it was now the opportune moment to exchange anything which only makes the white pawns so much stronger and his king safer. The right play seems to be 23...Bc5 24. Rxa1 c6 25. Bf4† Ka7 26. Nc7 Qd4 or 25. Nc3 Qd4 26. Rf1 Ka7 leaving him with 27. Qxc5 Qxc5 28. Be3 Qxe3† 29. Kxe3 Raf8 with good chances for the ending.

Analysis: after 29...Raf8

24.	Nxb4	Qd4
25.	Nc2	Nxc2
26.	Kxc2	Rg6
27.	Bd2	Rd6
28.	Rf3	Qa4†

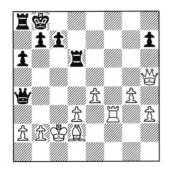

| 29. | Kc1 | .... |

Of course not 29. Kb1 on account of 29...Qd1†

29.	....	Qxa2
30.	Bc3	Rc6
31.	Qxh7	b5
32.	Qe7	Qb3
33.	Kd2	a5
34.	Rf5	Kb7
35.	Rc5	R8a6

36.	g5	Rxc5
37.	Qxc5	Rc6
38.	Qd5	Qa4
39.	g6	b4
40.	g7	....

The decisive manoeuvre. Nothing can stop the pawn, nor has the black queen any checks for the present.

40.	....	bxc3†
41.	bxc3	Qa3
42.	g8=Q	Qxc3†
43.	Ke2	Qc2†
44.	f3	Qd1†
45.	Kg3	Qg1†
46.	Kh4	Qf2†
47.	Kh5	Qf3†
48.	Qg4	Qf6
49.	Q4f5	Qh6†
50.	Kg4	Qg7†
51.	Qg5	

1-0

At last the moment has arrived—which by necessity had to arrive sooner or later, the black rook being pinned where the checks have exhausted themselves, and Black therefore resigns the hopeless fight.

Let us now return to white's 14th move and see what Lasker had to say.

Analysis: after 14. Bg5

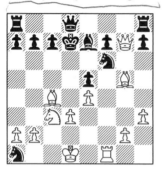

14. Bg5 is Lasker's suggestion in place of 14. Qxf7 as played in the game.

Lasker examines:
(A) 14...Qf8
(B) 14...Kc8
(C) 14...Rg8

Variation A

| 14. | .... | Qf8[g8] |
| 15. | Bxf6 | .... |

will follow and the exchange of queens will turn out to the advantage of White, as the black knight at a1 is virtually lost.

Variation B

| 14. | .... | Kc8 |

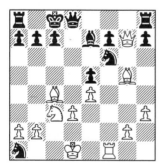

| 15. | Bxf6 | Bxf6 |

16.	Rxf6	Rg8
17.	Qxh7	Rxg2
18.	Qf5†	Kb8

Or 18...Qd7 19. Be6.

| 19. | Rxf7 | Rg8 |
| 20. | Qxe5 | |

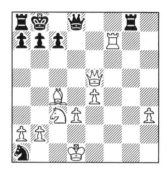

And Black is quite helpless.

Variation C

| 14. | .... | Rg8 |
| 15. | Qxf7 | .... |

Now four sub-variations:
(C1) 15...Rxg5
(C2) 15...Qf8
(C3) 15...Rf8
(C4) 15...Kc8

Variation C1

| 15. | .... | Rxg5 |

102

| 16. | Qe6† | Ke8 |
| 17. | Rxf6 | .... |

Threatening mate in two by 18. Rf8† etc.

| 17. | .... | Rg7 |
| 18. | Nd5 | .... |

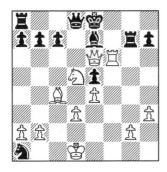

| 18. | .... | c6 |

Or 18...Qd6 19. Nxc7† Qxc7 20. Bb5† Kd8 21. Rf8† Bxf8 22. Qe8 mate.

19.	Qxe5	Rc8
20.	Nxe7	Rxe7
21.	Rf8† [30]	....

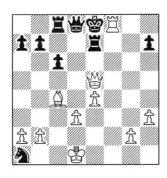

And should win.

Variation C2

| 15. | .... | Qf8 |
| 16. | Qe6† | Kd8[e8] |

17.   Rxf6

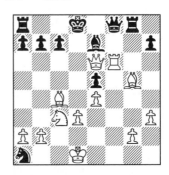

Variation C3

| 15. | .... | Rf8 |

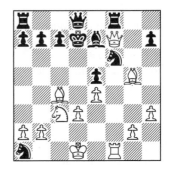

16.	Qe6†	Ke8
17.	Nd5	Nxd5
18.	Rxf8†	Kxf8
19.	Bxd5	Ke8
20.	Qf7†	Kd7
21.	Qf5†	

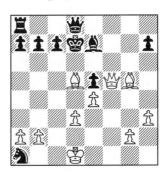

Wins the queen or mates.

Variation C4

15.	....	Kc8
16.	Bxf6	Rf8
17.	Bxe7	Rxf7
18.	Rxf7	

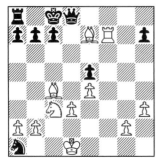

Speedily regaining the queen.

This is a rather complex piece of analysis and not surprisingly a few chinks have been found. Before we get too far along it seems appropriate to hear what Tchigorin had to say.

At the board 14. Bg5 was considered but then rejected in view of 14...Nh5 15. Qxf7 Qe8 16. Bxe7 Qxe7 17. Qxh5 Raf8.

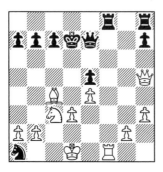

To Tchigorin it looked like Black was working out of his difficulties. However, Vasyukov and Nikitin (in their book on Tchigorin) point out the move 18. Rf5! when "Black's position remains difficult." However, Tchigorin,

Vasyukov and Nikitin all seem to have missed a decisive, earlier improvement,

Analysis: after 15...Qe8

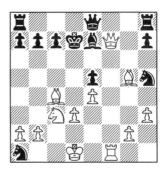

namely 16. Qe6+! Kd8 17. Bb5! c6 18. Rf7!, when Black faces mate or ruinous material loss.

Returning to Lasker's main line (Variation C1) 14. Bg5 Rg8 15. Qxf7 Rxg5 16. Qe6† Ke8 17. Rxf6 Rg7 18. Nd5

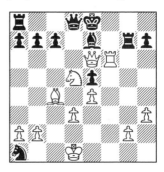

Tchigorin took issue with Lasker's parenthetical note 18...Qd6 19. Nxc7†

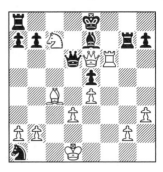

Replacing 19...Qxc7? with 19...Kd8 20. Qxd6† Bxd6 21. Nxa8 Bc5 22. g4 h5 23. Rf7 (what else?) 23...Rxf7 24. Bxf7 hxg4 25. hxg4 Be3 26. Be6 Bg5

when despite the two-pawn advantage it's hard to see how White makes progress. The kings on both sides are tied down, preventing the knights in the corners from getting out.

Young Savielly Tartakower added his two cents' worth some ten years later, taking Lasker's main line out to move nineteen before demonstrating his "improvement."

14. Bg5 Rg8 15. Qxf7 Rxg5 16. Qe6† Ke8 17. Rxf6 Rg7 18. Nd5 c6 19. Qxe5

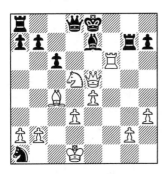

In place of Lasker's 19...Rc8, Tartakower gave 19...Qb8! ready to answer (a) 20. Nc7† with 20...Qxc7! 21. Qxc7 Bxf6, while (b) 20. Qh5† can be met by 20...Kd8 21. Nxe7 Qh2!

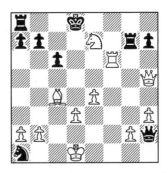

However, Tartakower seems not have considered 22. Nxc6†!!, when it appears White comes out ahead after either 23...Kc7 (if 23...Kd7 it's mate in 13 starting with 24. Ne5†) 24.Qa5† b6 25. Qe5† Qxe5 26. Nxe5, or 23...bxc6 24. Rf8† Kd7 24. Qf5† Kc7 25. Qa5† Kd7 26. Rxa8, since now if 26...Qg1† 27. Qe1.

All very messy. We give the last analytical comment to the *Deutsche Schachzeitung* where an improvement for White is proposed at move 18. So we run up: 14. Bg5 Rg8 15. Qxf7 Rxg5 16. Qe6† Ke8 17. Rxf6 Rg7 and now 18. Qxe5 (instead of Lasker's 18. Nd5) 18...c6 (to stop 19. Nd5) but there's something else afoot: 19. Rf3!

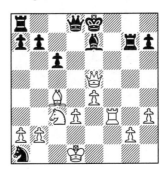

when the g7-rook cannot run to safety because of 20. Rf8†!

We'll give the final word to Marco who

was at Hastings both as participant and as a reporter. He recounts the following amusing incident:

"Tchigorin, in promoting his pawn (move 42), instead of a queen placed an upside-down rook at g8, and then proceeded to an adjoining room in order to obtain a white queen. En route he ran into Lasker, who, quickly meeting him half-way and taking into account that White had yet another two irresistible passed pawns on the board, handed him three queens with the words, "I trust, Mr. Tchigorin, that these will be enough for you!"

Game #32
Steinitz vs. Schlechter
Hastings Rd. 2, 1895
Giuoco Piano

1.	e4	e5
2.	Nf3	Nc6
3.	Bc4	Bc5
4.	c3	Nf6
5.	d4	exd4
6.	cxd4	Bb4†
7.	Nc3	Nxe4
8.	0-0	Bxc3
9.	bxc3	d5
10.	Ba3	

A novelty by the leader of the white forces. White intends to give up the

piece in order to prevent Black from castling into safety.

10.	....	Be6

Black declines the acceptance of the sacrifice with doubtful judgment. If 10...dxc4, the consequences might be 11. Re1 f5 12. Nd2 Kf7 13. Nxe4 fxe4 14. Rxe4 Qf6. This appears to be the only possible move as 14...Re8 would be answered by 15. Qh5† and 14...Bf5 by 15. Rf4. 15. Qe2

Analysis: after 15. Qe2

(a) 15...Be6? 16. Re1 Rhe8 17. d5 and wins.

(b) 15...Bd7? 16. Qxc4† Kg6 17. d5[31] Ne5 18. Qxc7 Rhe8 19. Qxb7[32] with three pawns for the piece.

(c) 15...Bf5! 16. Rf4 h5 17. Qxc4† Kg6 18. d5 Ne5 19. Qxc7 Rhe8 and although Black is two pawns behind for the piece and may lose a third, his attack is excellent.

11.	Bb5	Nd6
12.	Bxc6†	bxc6
13.	Ne5	0-0
14.	Nxc6	Qf6

Black plays exceedingly well for position. It is with best judgment that he allows White the opportunity of doubling his d-pawn, and White is wise to abstain from it, as by doing so he would involve both his knight and his c-pawn in difficulties.

15.	Rb1	Bf5

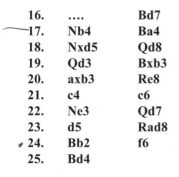

16.	Rb3	....

The rook ought to have left the open file, as 16. Rb4 would be answered by 16...a5; and the move actually made loses the exchange for a pawn.

16.	....	Bd7
17.	Nb4	Ba4
18.	Nxd5	Qd8
19.	Qd3	Bxb3
20.	axb3	Re8
21.	c4	c6
22.	Ne3	Qd7
23.	d5	Rad8
24.	Bb2	f6
25.	Bd4	

A poor place for the bishop. It seems as though 25. Ba3 would give him better prospects of fixing his pawns far ahead in the camp of his adversary.

25.	....	Nc8
26.	Rd1	Nb6
27.	d6	....

A faulty combination, which by opening up all lines to the rooks endangers White's game to a considerable extent.

White probably expected to win a piece in case the pawn was captured, but overlooked the retort of Black's 29th move regaining the piece immediately.

The remaining moves were:

27.	....	Qxd6
28.	c5	Qe6
29.	cxb6	c5
30.	bxa7	Rxd4
31.	Qc2	Rxd1†
32.	Qxd1	Qf7
33.	h4	Qxa7
34.	h5	h6
35.	Nf5	Qc7
36.	g3	Qc6
37.	Kh2	Kh8
38.	Qg4	Qd7
39.	Qf3	Re5
40.	Nh4	Kg8
41.	Ng6	Re8

42.	Nf4	Rb8
43.	Qe4	Qf7
44.	Qf5	Qxb3
45.	Qxc5	Qb5
46.	Qc7	Re8
47.	Kg2	Rb8
48.	Kh2	Re8
49.	Kg2	

½-½

Lasker does not comment on the final half of the game, since Schlechter, the exchange ahead, made no serious attempt to win.

However, the final position with White well entrenched on the kingside does indeed look drawn.

The opening variation 10. Ba3, whereby Steinitz tried to revive Greco's Attack (the pre-Möller days), is of some interest, and was played twice by Steinitz against Lasker in their return match. Lasker won both games.

Game #33
Schlechter - von Bardeleben
Hastings Rd. 8, 1895
Ruy Lopez

1.	e4	e5
2.	Nf3	Nc6
3.	Bb5	a6
4.	Ba4	Nf6

5.	Nc3	

5. 0-0 followed by 6. d4 seems to take better advantage of the useless advance of the black a-pawn.

5.	....	Bc5
6.	Nxe5	

The only feasible continuation that promises attack. If for instance, 6. 0-0 d6 7. d3 b5 8. Bb3 Bg4, Black will certainly not have the worst of the position.

6.	....	Nxe5
7.	d4	Bd6
8.	0-0	0-0
9.	f4	

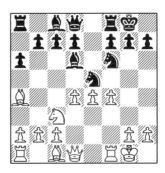

This early advance strains the position to an extent which is not justified by the disposition of forces. It would have been simpler and far preferable to take the knight immediately, and then to continue by 10. Qd3.

9.	....	Nc4
10.	e5	Be7
11.	exf6	Bxf6
12.	d5	....

White's game is now anything but comfortable. Black will be first to take the open e-file with his rooks in the ordinary course of events, for instance 12. Nd5 b5 13. Bb3 Bb7 14. Nxf6† Qxf6 15. Bxc4 bxc4 16. Be3 Rfe8 17. Qd2 Be4 etc., and will then, of course, have everything his own way, the advance of the f-pawn having left that file very weak. White therefore prefers to run great risks in order to be able to assume the attack.

12.	....	c5

He threatens 13...Bxc3 14. bxc3 b5 15. Bb3 Nb6 etc., and if 13. Bb3 Nd6 14. a4 c4 15. Ba2 b5.

13.	Ne4	Bxb2
14.	Bxb2	Nxb2
15.	Qh5	Nxa4
16.	f5	f6
17.	Rf4	Qe8
18.	Nxf6†	gxf6
19.	Qg4†	Kh8
20.	Re4	Qf7
21.	Rae1	d6
22.	Re7	Bd7

Perfectly incomprehensible. So far he has correctly met the attack and need only remove his queen to g8 to earn the reward for his circumspect play, e.g. 22...Qg8 23. Qxa4 Bxf5 24. Rxb7 Rae8 25. R1e7 Rxe7 26. Rxe7 Qxd5 and should win. Or 23. Qh3 Nb6 threatening ...Nxd5 or ...Nd7 and ...Ne5 with

the same result. It must be admitted, however, that even in the text variation White's play to draw is exceedingly difficult to find.

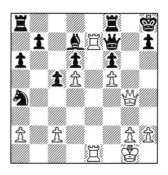

23.	Rxf7	Rxf7
24.	Re6	

A very interesting manoeuvre. The rook must eventually be taken as otherwise the d-pawn would fall. The passed pawn at e6 which White thus obtains is quite sufficient a compensation for the exchange sacrificed.

24.	....	Rg7
25.	Qh4	Bxe6
26.	dxe6	Nb6
27.	Qxf6	Nd5
28.	Qb2	Kg8

He has nothing else. 28...Rf8 would have been answered by 29. e7 Nxe7 [33] 30. f6.

29.	f6	Nxf6

Of course the only alternative open to him, as otherwise he would have to lose one of his rooks. The game is now perfectly equalized and legitimately ends in a draw.

30.	Qxf6	Rf8
31.	Qh4	Re8

32.	Qf6	Rf8
33.	Qh4	Re8
34.	Qf6	

½-½

Game #34
Tchigorin vs. Steinitz
Hastings Rd. 13, 1895
Evans Gambit

1.	e4	e5
2.	Nf3	Nc6
3.	Bc4	Bc5
4.	b4	Bxb4
5.	c3	Ba5
6.	0-0	d6
7.	d4	exd4

(Tucked away in Common Sense *was Lasker's little bombshell 7...Bb6 — BA)*

8.	cxd4	Nf6
9.	e5	dxe5
10.	Ba3	Be6

So far everything is book. It has always been the opinion that Black, although two pawns ahead, will not be able to develop his pieces, as castling kingside is prevented, and the king dare not occupy the centre any length of time. Black seemed to believe that he may get his king safely castled to the queen's side, but this game does not corroborate such an opinion, in spite of the success which attended that manoeuvre in this instance.

11.	Bb5	....

Tchigorin's favorite post for the bishop in the Evans Gambit.

11.	....	Qd5
12.	Qa4	0-0-0
13.	Bxc6	bxc6

14.	Bc5	Bb6
15.	Qa6†	....

White ultimately wins the exchange by this manoeuvre, but at an enormous expense. It would have been better to leave things as they were and to continue simply with 15. Nxe5. If then 15...Nd7 16. Nxc6 must win the exchange in favorable position; and if 15...Ne4 16. Bxb6 cxb6 17. Qxa7 will equalize material forces, with the position to White's advantage.

15.	....	Kb8
16.	Nxe5	Nd7
17.	Nc3	Nxc5
18.	Qe2	Qd6
19.	dxc5	Qxc5
20.	Na4	Qb5
21.	Qxb5	cxb5

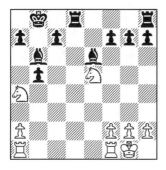

22.	Nxb6	axb6
23.	Nc6†	Kb7
24.	Nxd8†	Rxd8
25.	a3	c5
26.	f3	Kc6
27.	Rfd1	Ra8

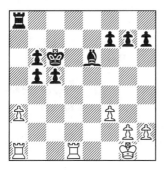

A rook being very well qualified to support advancing pawns and to check the approach of the hostile king, it is judicious play to avoid its exchange for the present.

28.	Kf2	Ra4
29.	Ke3	h5

Advancing these pawns, which constitute the only weakness in Black's camp, protects them against any possible attack of the rooks or king.

30.	Kd2	b4
31.	axb4	Rxb4
32.	Rdb1	Rxb1

Now it is just as well to simplify, two united passed pawns with the support of the king and bishop being more than a match for king and rook. Black need only take care to leave the passed pawns as much as possible on the colour not dominated by the bishop—i.e. on black squares.

33.	Rxb1	b5
34.	Ra1	b4
35.	Kc2	Kd5
36.	Rd1†	Kc4
37.	Rd8	Bd5
38.	h4	Kd4
39.	Rb8	Be6
40.	Rb7	g6
41.	Rb5	b3†
42.	Kb2	c4
43.	Rb4	Kd3
44.	Rb6	c3†
45.	Kb1	Ke3

0-1

Threatening 46...Bf5†. 46. g4 would be answered by 46...Kxf3. White is therefore perfectly helpless.

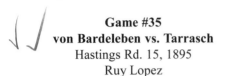

Game #35
von Bardeleben vs. Tarrasch
Hastings Rd. 15, 1895
Ruy Lopez

1.	e4	e5
2.	Nf3	Nc6
3.	Bb5	a6
4.	Ba4	Nf6
5.	0-0	d6

This defence leaves Black with a somewhat cramped position, if White continues with 6. d4 Bd7 7. dxe5 dxe5 8. Nc3 Bd6 9. Bg5 Ne7 10. Bb3.

| 6. | Nc3 | .... |

A mistake. White having castled ought to immediately open the centre by 6. d4. Now he comes into difficulties.

| 6. | .... | b5 |
| 7. | Bb3 | Bg4 |

| 8. | Ne2 | .... |

It is hard to see how he could prevent the threatened ...Nd4 in any other way. The alternative would have been 8. h3 Bh5 9. g4 Bg6 (It is remarkable that in this position the sacrifice of the knight against two pawns is bad. If 9...Nxg4 10. hxg4 Bxg4 11. Bd5! Nd4 12. Nxe5 Bxd1 13. Bxf7† Ke7 14. Nd5 mate.) 10. d3 Na5, whereupon Black appears to have slightly the better position.

8.	....	Bxf3
9.	gxf3	Qd7
10.	a4	Qh3

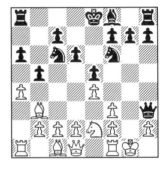

A splendid and profound combination. Its idea is illustrated by the following two moves of Black. Had White seen it, he probably would have played 10. c3 Qh3 11. Ng3 h5 12. d4 with a good game, as the sacrifice of 12...Ng4 13. hxg4 hxg4 would fail on account of 14. Re1.

| 11. | axb5 | h5 |
| 12. | Re1 | .... |

He must provide (in view of the threatened Ng4) an escape for his king. Suppose instead 12. bxc6 Ng4 13. fxg4 hxg4 14. Re1 Qxh2† 15. Kf1 Qh3† 16. Kg1 Qh1 mate.

| 12. | .... | Ng4 |

Schallopp offers 12...Ne7!! 13. bxa6 Ng6 etc. or 13. Rxa6 Rb8[d8] 14. Ra3 Ng6 as the winning line. However, in the latter variation, he fails to consider the saving 14. Ng3! (instead of 14. Ra3), e.g. 14...Ng6 15. Bc4 Nf4 16. Bf1, or 14...h4 15. Nf1 Ng6 16. Ne3 Nf4 17. Bc4 and 18. Bf1, with a winning material advantage. — BA.

13.	hxg4	hxg4

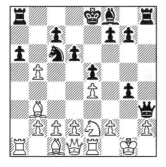

14.	Bxf7†	....

The only possible means to avert disaster. 14. Ng3 instead would not answer that purpose, as the consequence would be 14. Ng3 Nd4 15. Re3 Qxh2† 16. Kf1 Qh1† 17. Nxh1 Rxh1† 18. Kg2 Rxd1 19.Rxa6[34] Rb8 20. Ba4 Nf3 winning in such or similar manner in any variation White may choose.

14.	....	Kxf7
15.	Ra3	Qxh2†
16.	Kf1	....

16.	....	axb5

It is here that Black misses his chance. The move actually made is elegant, but not sufficiently strong. He should have taken advantage of the momentary dislocation of the white pieces in the following manner: 16...Nd4. This threatens ...Nf3. White has, therefore only two alternatives: 17. Nxd4 Qh1† 18. Ke2 Qxe4† 19. Re3 Qxd4 20. bxa6 Be7 21. Rh1 Bg5 22. Rxh8 Rxh8 23. c3 Qd5 and the result of the game cannot be doubtful, as White must lose the exchange at the very least. Or White may continue at his 17th turn: 17. Ng1 Be7 18. Qxg4 Bh4 19. Nh3 (19. Qg2 would lose on account of 19...Qxg2† 20. Kxg2 Nxc2 etc.) 19...Raf8 whereupon White has no sufficient defence. Suppose, for instance, 20. bxa6 Qh1†[35] 21. Ng1 Kg8.

17.	Rg3	Rh6
18.	d3	....

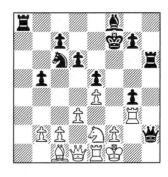

18.	....	Rf6

Here 18...Ra1 suggests itself. If, then, 19. Ng1 Rf6 20. Rg2 Qh4 21. Qxg4 Qxg4 22. Rxg4 Nb4 winning either the c- or d-pawn. But 19. c3, threatening Qb3† would have been a sufficient reply.

19.	Be3	Be7
20.	Rg2	Qh4
21.	Ng3	Rf3

| 22. | Ke2 | .... |

All these manoeuvres are excellent. White brings his king into safety on the queenside, and will soon be able to assume the attack against the opened king-side of Black. Black's extra pawn at g4 is of no permanent value, being indefensible in the long run.

22.	....	Qf6
23.	Nf5	Rh3
24.	Kd2	Rh7
25.	Qxg4	Bf8

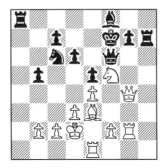

| 26. | Qf3 | .... |

Now it is White who has, without a doubt, the better game. It would have been advisable to double the rooks on the g-file, and afterwards proceed with Rg3 and Rf3. Black seems to have no defence against this manoeuvre. Suppose, for instance, 26. Reg1 Ra2 27.

Rg3 Rxb2 28. Rf3 Ke8 29. Bg5 Qg6 30. Nxg7† and mates in a few more moves.

26.	....	Ke8
27.	Reg1 [36]	Qf7
28.	Qg4	Ne7
29.	Nh4	Ng8
30.	Ng6	Nf6
31.	Qf5	Ng8
32.	Qxf7† [37]	Kxf7

After this exchange of queens the draw become the natural and legitimate result.

33.	Rf1	Be7
34.	Nxe7	Kxe7
35.	R2g1	Kd7
36.	Ra1	Rxa1
37.	Rxa1	Ne7
38.	Ra7	Rh2
39.	Ke2 [38]	Nc6
40.	Ra1	Ke6
	½-½	

Analytical Endnotes

by Taylor Kingston

In the course of proofreading the manuscript for this book, I followed my usual practice of playing through all the games and notes with the computer program *Fritz8* in "infinite analysis" mode. The main purpose of this was to check the accuracy of the notation (typographical errors, illegal moves, misnumbering, etc.), but an interesting byproduct was that a number of analytical errors were found, of both omission and commission. Some are relatively minor, occasions where Lasker gives a good move but misses a more quickly decisive one. Some, however, are more serious: instances where Lasker calls a bad move good, a good move bad, or he overlooks a strong move that would change the complexion of the game. All told, I found thirty-eight such instances that I felt deserved mention.

Three questions then arose:

(a) Should the errors be pointed out?
(b) If so, in what fashion?
(c) How could a World Champion make that many mistakes?

To question (a), I think Lasker himself would have been the first to say yes; his objectivity and lack of egotism on such matters were legendary. And he would certainly agree that an author and publisher have an obligation not to mislead their readers, however inadvertently.

For question (b), it was felt that it would do the reader a disservice to disrupt the flow of Lasker's prose and ideas with interruptions in mid-course. Therefore we chose to make the corrections as unobtrusive as possible, using only superscripted numbers (e.g. [23]) to mark their presence within the text of the book.

For question (c), several possibilities come to mind. One, *Common Sense in Chess* is first and foremost a book of ideas, of general principles, not exhaustive analysis. Lasker felt that for inexperienced players, for whom this book is intended, mazes of variations were just so much "mental ballast." He almost certainly did not expend the same effort on this lecture series for club players as he did on his more serious analytical efforts, such as the tournament book *St. Petersburg 1909*. Two, considering his busy schedule during 1894-96 (two World Championship matches, three major tournaments, and extensive exhibition tours in America and Europe), it's a minor miracle that he had time to write a book at all. Three, the Lasker of 1894-95, when the book was written, had by no means reached the height of his powers. Chess skill bloomed later in those days.

Four, Lasker may have *deliberately* left some errors in, to reward the student who investigates for himself. We recommend that the reader take such an approach — when you see a superscript in the notation (e.g. 12. Ne2[1] Bxg5 in the Fritz-Mason game), try first to figure out for yourself what better move may be possible there.

Five, some of these errors *are* rather difficult to ferret out. Some were during play by some of the greatest masters of all time: Morphy, Anderssen, Tarrasch, Schlechter, Lasker himself. They eluded analysts for decades. Some involve the sort of "funny move" a brute-force computer considers, but is unlikely to occur to a human master.

Lastly, there is simply the clichéd but inescapable fact: *errare humanum est*. As we saw in the recent Kramnik-*Fritz* match, even World Champions can overlook something as basic as mate-in-one (though nothing that egregious occurs here).

Does all this mean that *Common Sense in Chess* is not a good book? Absolutely not. It remains an instructional classic — but its instructional value will be increased if the reader approaches it with the skeptical attitude Lasker himself always took at the chess board.

1) 12. Ne2

Stronger is 12. Qd3†! f5 (if 12...Kh5 13. g4† Kxg4 14. Qf3#) 13. exf6† Kxf6 14. Qf3† Kg6 15. h5† Kxg5 (15...Kh6 16. Qd3 Rf5 17. Nxe6) 16. Qg3† Kf5 17. Qg6† Kf4 18. Ne2#

2) 9...0-0

The natural move, loses prettily as Lasker demonstrates. Less natural and less pretty is 9...Kf8, but it allows Black to hang on.

3) 8. Nd5

8. Nd5? is an oversight, losing a piece to 8...Nbd4!. White must play 8. Nxb5 instead.

4) 13...d5

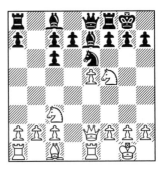

13...f6 seems to equalize.

5) 15. Nh7

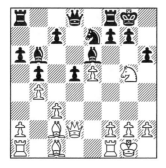

Rather than 15. Nh7, White should consider 15. Nxe6 fxe6 16. Qd3.

6) 17...f5

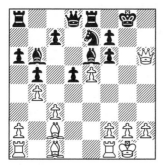

Much better is 17...Ng6! 18. Bxg6 fxg6 19. Qxg6† Kh8. White can force a draw here by 20. Qh6† Kg8 21. Qg6† etc. If he tries for more, 20. exf6, Black can defend by 20...Qd7 and 21...Qh7.

7) 23...Qg7

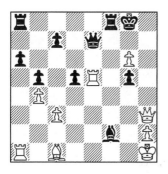

23...Qg7? is a mistake, while 23...g4! maintains equality. (a) 24. Qxg4? Qxe5 (b) 24. Rxe7 gxh3; (c) 24.Qh6 Qg7; (d) 24.Bg5 Qg7; (e) 24.Qh5 Qh4 25.Rxd5 Qxh5 26.Rxh5 Kg7.

8) 16...Bd7

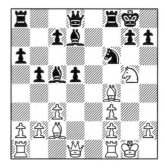

On 17. Be5, Black defends with 17...c6. He need not fear 18. Bxf6 Qxf6 19. Nxh7 as 19...Qh4 20. Nxf8 Rxf8 yields an excellent attack. Stronger is 17.Nxh7! which wins a pawn, or more after 17...Nxh7 18. Qxd5† Kh8 19. Qh5 etc.

9) 27. f6

27. f6 is best answered by 27...g5! Stronger therefore is 27. Rf3! Qxa6 28. Rh3 h6 29. Bxh6.

10) 29. Ra3

White need not retreat 29. Ra3. Instead, 29. Rf3! Qxa6 30. Rh3 and Black has only a few spite checks to delay Qxh7 mate.

11) 15...d5

15...Qf5! improves, though after 16.Rd3! g5 17.Nh4! gxh4 18.Rf3 Qxf3 19.gxf3, White is probably still winning.

12) 16...Kf8

Black has a good alternative in 16...Nxd6 17.exd6† Qe6. If 18. Qxe6† fxe6 19. Nd2 Bxd4†, or 18. Ne5 Nxe5 19. dxe5 Bxe5.

13) 18. Bd6

Long ago Steinitz showed that 18. Bd6 should be answered with 18...Qxa1† 19. Ke2 Qb2! and Black successfully defends. Instead of 18. Bd6, White has three alternatives: 18. d4, 18. Be3, 18. Re1, all of which have claims to winning.

14) 11. g4

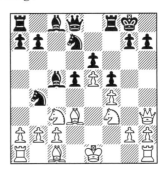

11. Ng5! attacking e6/h7 wins on the spot. Black's previous move, 10...Nb4? is never played precisely for this reason. He normally continues 10...Nd4 or 10...Re8, guarding e6.

15) 14. Nxd5

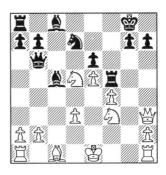

14. Nxd5 can be answered by 14...Qc6! 15. d4 (or 15. Nc3 Nxe5!) 15...Qxd5 16. dxc5 Nxe5! and Black is winning.

16) 12. g4

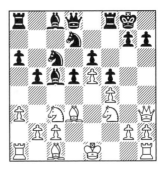

Again overlooking 12. Ng5! Black should play 11...Be7 (or ...Nb6) as 11....b5? is a mistake.

17) 16...Nd7

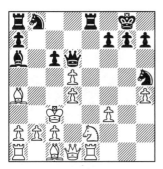

Stronger 16...Qxd5! threatening ...Qxf3† and ...Qc4†.

18) 18...Rac8

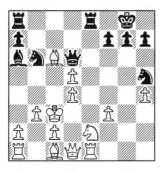

The computer finds a subtle objection to this move and prefers 18...Rec8! See next two notes.

19) 19. Kd2
Assume 18...Rec8 was played and White continued 19. Kd2 as in the game. Black wins by Morphy's method using a different introduction, 19...Qh6†.

If 20. Kc3 Nxd5† and 21...Qxc6. So the play goes 20. f4 Nxf4 21. Nxf4 Qxf4†:

(a) 22. Re3 Nxd5 23. Bxd5 Qf2† 24. Re2 Bxe2 25. Qxe2 Rxc2†.
(b) 22. Kc3 Qd6, threatens 23...Nxd5† and we're back in Morphy lines. 23. Kb2 (23. Kd2 Rxc6 24. dxc6 Qxd4#) 23...Rxc6 24. dxc6 Na4† etc.

20) 21. Rxe2

The bishop is pinned and White need not rush to take it. Instead, he can improve his defensive posture: 21. c3, 21. a4, 21. Kb1. Had 18...Rec8 been played there would be no pin in the sequence 19. Kb2 Rxc6 20. dxc6 Bxe2 (here he has to take) 21. Q(R)xe2 Na4† etc.

21) 19...Rxc6

Another way is 19...Nxd5.
(a) 20. c4 Qxc6, if 21. cxd5 Rxe2† 22. Rxe2 Qc3#.
(b) 20. Bxd5 Qb4† 21. c3 Rxe2† 22. Qxe2 Qxc3† 23. Kd1 Bxe2† and 24...Qxa1.
(c) 20. Bxe8 Bxe2

119

(c1) 21.Qxe2 Qf4† 22. Qe3 Nxe3 or 22. Kd1 Nc3#
(c2) 21. Rxe2 Qb4† 22. Kd3 Rc3† 23. Ke4 Qe7† 24. Kf5 (24. Kxd5 Nf6#) 24...Qf6† 25. Kg4 (25. Ke4 Qe6#) 25...Qxf3† 26. Kg5 h6#

On a practical level Morphy's 19...Rxc6 is easier to calculate (less variations) and more than convincing.

22) 21. Rxe2

Here too the bishop is pinned. The threat of 21...Qxd4# precludes alternative measures. (a) 21. Kc3 Qxc6† (b) 21. c4 Qxd4† (c) 21. c3 Qf4† (d) 21. Bb2 Qf4† 22. Kc3 Nd5#

23) 23...Bh3†

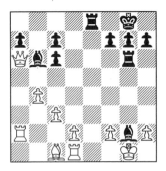

Quicker was 23...Be4† 24.Kf1 Bf5! 25.Qe2 Bh3† 26.Ke1 Rg1#. This forced mate was pointed out by J.H. Bauer, Lasker's victim in game #12, the famous double bishop sacrifice.

24) 16...Rhe8

16...Rhe8 is a mistake, refuted by 17. Rf1! Qg6 18. Nf6 Qxg7 19. Nxe8 Rxe8 20. Rxf7. The correct move is 16...Rhg8! and in comparable lines Black plays ...Rxg7.

25) 26. Be2

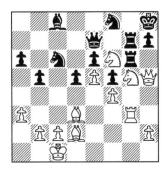

"White misses here a fine opportunity of carrying the day by 26. Ngxh7! and if 26...Rxh7 27. Rxg6 threatening mate and wins."—Steinitz, *International Chess Magazine* for October 1888. Burn could and should have averted this by sacrificing the exchange one move sooner, 25...Rxf6.

26) 34. Be3 (after 33...Qe4†)

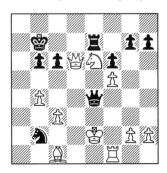

White can better play 34. Kf2! Qxf5† 35. Kg3!
(a) after 35...Qxe6 36. Qxe6 Rxe6 37. Bxb2 Re2 38. Rf2 he safely keeps his material. Had White played 35. Kg1 then at the end Black causes problems

with 37...Re2 38. Rf2 Re1† 39. Rf1 Re2 controlling the second rank.

(b) Lively complications set in on 35...Qg6† White must return his piece, 36. Ng5! Re5 37. h4 Nd3 38. Bd2 fxg5, but 39. Qd7† Ka6 (39...Kb8 40. Rf8†) 40. c4! develops a mating attack. On the further moves 40...gxh4† 41. Kh2 Qg3† 42. Kg1, Black runs out of resources, and the rook enters, at a1 or f7, (after Qc8†).

27) 40....Nc6

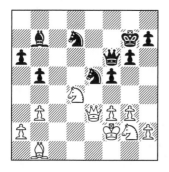

40...Bxf3!, wins a pawn, since if 41. Nxf3 Ng4†

28) 42...Qe5

Once again missing 42...Nce5! 43. Nd4 Bxf3!

29) 7. Kh3

The paranthetical suggestion 7. Kh3? loses to 7...Ke1! 9. Kg2 Ke2 9. Kg3 Kf1

10. Kh3 Kf2 etc. The only correct move is 7. Kh1.

30) 21. Rf8†

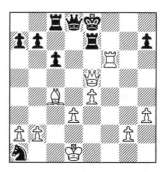

White can force mate with 21. Bf7† Kf8 22. Be6† Ke8 23. Qh5† Rf7 24. Qxf7#.

31) 17. d5

White does better to avoid 17. d5 in favor of 17. Re3, aiming to draw after 17...Rae8 18. Rg3† Kh5 19. Qd5† Qf5 20. Rh3† Kg6 21. Rg3† etc.

32) 19. Qxb7

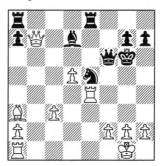

Continuing after 19. Qxb7 Black has the surprising 19...Nd3! 20. Re7 (if 20. Be7 Qxf2† 21. Kh1 Bh3 22. Rg1 Bf5 23. Rc4 Qb6) 20...Rxe7 21. Bxe7 Qxf2† 22. Kh1 Qb6! and wins, since if 23. Qxa8?? Nf2† 24.Kg1 Nh3† 25.Kh1 Qg1† 26.Rxg1 Nf2, smothered mate.

33) 29...Nxe7

29...Re8! If 30. f6 Rf7. Or 30. c4 Rexe7 31. cxd5 Re5 and two rooks are a match for the queen.

34) 19. Rxa6
The computer prefers 19. bxa6 retaining the rook on the first rank to defend the bishop.

35) 20...Qh1†

Most convincing is 20...Bxf2! 21. Nxf2 Ke8 (better than 21...Kg8 as the h-rook must be ready to play to f8).

(a) 22. Qc8† Ke7 23. Qxc7† Ke6 24. Qc4† Kd7 25. Qa4† Ke7 and the checks run out.
(b) 22. Qg2(g1) Rxf2† 23. Qxf2 Qh1† 24. Qg1 Rf8† and mate next move.
(c) 22. Re2 Qh1† 23. Qg1 Qxg1† 24. Kxg1 Nxe2† 25. Kf1 Nxc1.

36) 27. Reg1

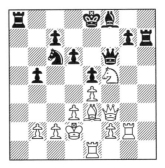

27. Nxg7†! gains a pawn and intensifies the attack. If 27...Bxg7 28.Qxf6 Bxf6 29. Rg8†, winning the a8-rook. On the previous move 26...Kg8 was preferable to the text 26...Ke8.

37) 32. Qxf7†

White wins a pawn by 32. Ra1! Rd8 (32...Rxa1?? 33. Qc8#) 33. Qxf7† Kxf7 34. Ra7 Rd7(c8) 35. Rb7 (or 35. Bb6) etc.

38) 39. Ke2

39. Bb6! wins the c-pawn, since if
39...Kc6 40. Ba5! Rxf2†? 41. Ke3,
threatening both 42. Kxf2 and 42.
Rxc7#. On his previous move Black
should have played 38...Rh8 or 38...g6.

Summary of Tournament Results 1889-1936

Year		Place	Won	Lost	Draw
1889	Breslau Happtunier A	1st	7	0	2
1889	Breslau Finals	1-2	4	2	0
1889	Amsterdam	2nd	5	1	2
1890	Berlin	1-2	6	1	1
1890	Graz	3rd	3	1	2
1892	London (B.C.A)	1st	8	1	2
1892	London (Masters)	1st	5	0	3
1893	New York	1st	13	0	0
1895	Hastings	3rd	14	4	3
1895/6	Saint Petersburg	1st	8	3	7
1896	Nuremberg	1st	12	3	3
1899	London	1st	19	1	7
1900	Paris	1st	14	1	1
1904	Cambridge Springs	2-3	9	2	4
1906	Trenton Falls	1st	4	0	2
1909	Saint Petersburg	1-2	13	2	3
1914	Saint Petersburg	1st	10	1	7
1918	Berlin	1st	3	0	3
1923	Mährisch Ostrau	1st	8	0	5
1924	New York	1st	13	1	6
1925	Moscow	2nd	10	2	8
1934	Zurich	5th	9	4	2
1935	Moscow	3rd	6	0	13
1936	Moscow	6th	3	5	10
1936	Nottingham	7-8	6	3	5

Summary of Match Results 1889-1921

(entries in **boldface** are World Championship matches)

Year		Won	Lost	Draw
1889	von Bardeleben, Berlin	2	1	1
1889/90	Mieses, Leipzig	5	0	3
1890	Bird, Liverpool	7	2	3
1890	Miniati, Manchester	3	0	2
1890	Englisch, Vienna	2	0	3
1892	Blackburne, London	6	0	4
1892	Bird, Newcastle on Tyne	5	0	0
1892/3	Showalter, Kokomo/Logansport	6	2	1
1893	Golmayo, Havana	2	0	1
1893	Vásquez, Havana	3	0	0
1893	Ettlinger, New York	5	0	0
1894	**Steinitz, NY/Phila/Montreal**	**10**	**5**	**4**
1896/7	**Steinitz, Moscow**	**10**	**2**	**5**
1901	Janowski, Manchester	1	0	1
1903	Tchigorin, Brighton (Rice Gambit)	1	2	3
1907	**Marshall, USA**	**8**	**0**	**7**
1908	**Tarrasch, Düsseldorf/Munich**	**8**	**3**	**5**
1908	Speijer, Amsterdam	2	0	1
1909	Janowski, Paris	2	2	0
1909	Janowski, Paris	7	1	2
1910	**Schlechter, Vienna/Berlin**	**1**	**1**	**8**
1910	**Janowski, Berlin**	**8**	**0**	**3**
1916	Tarrasch, Berlin	5	0	1
1921	**Capablanca, Havana**	**0**	**4**	**10**

Index of Players

(refers to game numbers)

Index of Openings

(refers to game numbers)